Born and brought up in Manchester, Andy Wood is a long time resident on Wirral. A lifelong devotee of the canals and inland waterways of Great Britain, he contributes to a number of magazines including "Waterways World", "Canal & Riverboat", "Best of British" and the "Wirral Champion Journal".

WIRRAL CAMERA OBSCURA

By

ANDY WOOD

First Published 2007 by Countyvise Limited,
14 Appin Road, Birkenhead, Wirral CH41 9HH.

British Library Cataloguing in Publication Data.
A catalogue record for this book is available from the British Library.

ISBN 978-1-901231-86-1

CONTENTS

'Waterways That Might Have Been" first appeared under the title 'Wirral Waterways' in the Wirral Champion Journal, Vol 13 No 3.

♦

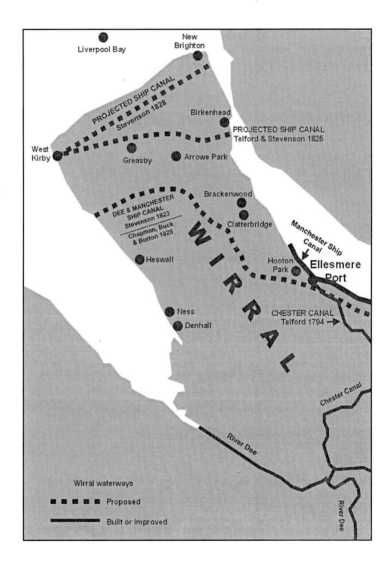

INTRODUCTION

I ask the reader to indulge my liking for metaphor; particularly that which provides the title for this book. Those of us who are of a certain age may, as small children, have been taken by fond parents to a Camera Obscura, (in my case it was at Eastbourne). If so, you will most probably recall entering a small, elevated cabin, perhaps on the roof of a seaside pier pavilion. No electronics, computer jiggery-pokery or even occult practices were involved but you could see, spread out on a circular table, an image from life of the surroundings. Light, as any physicist will tell you, travels in a straight line, and when some of the light reflected from a bright object passes through a small hole it does not scatter but crosses and forms an upside-down image on any flat surface that is held parallel to the hole. This is the principle used in the Camera Obscura. Both educative and entertaining, in the 19th Century with improved lenses capable of projecting larger and sharper images, the Camera Obscura was popular at the seaside and in other places with attractive or interesting scenery. Funnily enough, in the course of researching this book, I discovered that at one time Wirral did actually possess a camera obscura. It was erected in Birkenhead Park in 1849, two years after the park opened. Situated close to the lake it was operated by a Mr Crookes and lasted until 1874.

My Camera Obscura however is a metaphorical one; in 21st Century language, a virtual one. It is also capable, unlike its ancestors, of looking back in time (thanks to space-time components manufactured and supplied by A Einstein Gesellschaft, Ulm, Germany).

Imagine, if you will, that it is positioned somewhere fairly central on the Wirral Peninsula with a certain degree of elevation; the Storeton Ridge perhaps. From there, I invite you to peer at the magical image of the landscape, spread out across the projection table and, of course, to travel back in time. Like any good showman, I will lay before you various points of interest from our elevated perspective. I think you may be surprised at what is revealed; you will see and explore aspects of Wirral that, perhaps, you never knew before.

♦

1.

A PLACE FOR EVERYONE

The open grassland and woodlands of Arrowe Park were laid out on boulder clay farmland over a period of some fifty years after the land had been acquired in 1835 by John Ralph Shaw, a wealthy Liverpool warehouse owner. As Alan Brack says in his book "The Wirral", "...it is a sobering thought that it was once just one man's private garden"! John Shaw bought the land from the Trustees of Boteler's Free Grammar School, Warrington. His mother's brother, who was twice Mayor of Liverpool, also owned land in the area and the two estates eventually became one.

Between 1835 and 1844 John Shaw built a mansion in Elizabethan style, which he called Arrowe Hall. The word 'arrowe' does not, as might be thought, have anything to do with archery, instead it comes from the Norse word 'erg' which means pasture- or farm-land some distance away from a farmhouse.

In 1864 the house was extended and in 1876 – by which time the property had been inherited by Captain Otho Shaw – a billiards room and a conservatory were added. From his early adulthood, the Captain was a game hunter, who travelled all over the world shooting animals and birds; (how bizarre and barbaric that sounds to 21st Century ears!). So that he could display his collection he had to enlarge the house even more. The collection included eagles, vultures and lesser birds of prey, bison, black bears, elks, leopards, moose, panthers, yaks, and a variety of other animals including nine tigers, one of which was reputed to have killed and eaten men, women and children, as well as some 600 head of cattle, and which he had spent nine days and nights stalking. Otho Shaw was also an antiquary, and Arrowe Hall boasted a fine collection of glass, pottery and silver plate as well as watercolours, oil paintings and antique furniture.

Towards the end of the 19th Century the Arrowe estate, like many others on Wirral, was bought by Lord Leverhulme, whose ambition, at one time, appeared to be to buy up the whole peninsula! In turn, the land was bought from him by the Corporation of Birkenhead in 1927.

Although it is not the biggest public park in the country, it is certainly larger than Hyde Park in London and contains a full-size 18-hole golf course, pitches for football and cricket, and the picturesquely landscaped course of the Arrowe Brook, as well as rolling acres of meadow- and woodland that would not disgrace an aristocratic estate. In 1982, by which time Birkenhead Hospital was no longer adequate to serve the population of the town, the new 910-bed Arrowe Park hospital was built in the park. Large as it is, it occupies only a small proportion – fifteen acres – of the park's total of 425 acres (172 hectares).

Apart from having once hosted a qualifying round of the British Open Championship on the golf course, Arrowe Park secured its place in history when the 3rd International Jamboree of the Scout movement took place there in 1929, celebrating the twenty-first anniversary of the publication of "Scouting for Boys" by Robert Baden-Powell. The formal foundation of the Boy Scouts had actually taken place just four miles from Arrowe Park, on January 24th 1908 at the Birkenhead YMCA.

Above:
Arrowe Hall

Left:
Robet Baden-Powell

Much has been written by others about the 3rd International Jamboree, so it needs little more than a brief summary here. Forty thousand (according to some sources, fifty thousand) Scouts gathered in the park, representing 31 different countries within the British Empire and 41 other less fortunate countries. It was said to be the greatest international assembly of young people that the world had seen up to that time. It was also memorable for the fact that it rained almost continuously during the two weeks of the Jamboree so that the boulder clay which underlies the park could not absorb the rain, and the site became a sea of mud.

The Jamboree was formally opened on Wednesday 31st July 1929 by HRH the Duke of Connaught, third son of Queen Victoria and the President of the Scout Association. Baden-Powell, as the Chief Scout, blew on the same Kudu Horn (the horn of an African antelope) with which he had sounded reveille at the first ever Scout camp on Brownsea Island in Dorset. The Prince of Wales flew from London in a Westland Wapiti biplane to Hooton Park Aerodrome (see "From Saxon Thanes to Vauxhall Motors") to attend the Jamboree, and spent two nights in an ordinary Scout tent. Baden-Powell himself travelled to Birkenhead by train but returned home as the newly-ennobled Lord Baden-Powell of Gilwell in a brand new Rolls-Royce towing a luxury caravan, both of which had been presented to him by the Scouts of the world.

Arrowe Hall itself was used for many years by Birkenhead Corporation as a convalescent home. Still owned by the local authority, it now offers supported living for adults with learning disabilities as an alternative to the traditional residential home: tenants have more autonomy and choice over how they wish to receive support. The surrounding woods and glorious open spaces of the park would make the Hall a particularly pleasant place for anyone to live.

Now known as Arrowe Country Park, about 250 acres (101 hectares) of the park are open parkland and deciduous woodland, while formal areas and the golf course take up another 160 acres (64.7 hectares), with the hospital and its car parks taking up the remainder. The woodland is mostly made up of oak, ash and beech, with some conifers such as Scots Pine. Some of its more unusual trees include ornamental species such as Redwood, Cedar of Lebanon, Maidenhair and Indian Bean tree, which were planted by the Shaws. Frequently observed birds include the rooks, magpies, jays, nuthatches, tree creepers and great and lesser spotted woodpeckers that are found in most woodlands of any size on Wirral.

Some areas of grassland and the edges of woodlands are preserved as wildflower meadows, which attract butterflies such as the Small Heath, Skipper and Speckled Wood. The lake and the Arrowe Brook provide habitats for a number of species of birds including, for anyone with the patience to watch and wait long enough, the Kingfisher. Smaller ponds around the park provide breeding grounds for a variety of pond life including frogs, newts, damsel- and dragonflies. Situated as it is in the centre of Wirral, between rural and urban areas, the park is easily reached by public transport. It is yet another example of the democratisation of our society, that a formerly private pleasure ground is now maintained for the benefit of all.

◆

2.

SECRETS OF OUR ANCESTORS

The Mesolithic, or Middle Stone Age, period of human development occurred at the end of the last Ice Age over 10,000 years ago. It began at the end of the Palaeolithic period and then evolved into the Neolithic period when man began to domesticate plants and animals, and as a result developed from being a hunter-gatherer to living in settled communities.

Until very recently, archaeologists believed that Mesolithic people roamed the forested countryside in small groups, hunting animals and gathering edible plants, roots, nuts and fruit in tune with the seasons. This bucolic image was based primarily on studies of modern peoples who still forage and hunt as a way of life. The latest research, however, casts doubt on this view. Far from having a fairly relaxed way of life, in which they had easy pickings, it seems that our hunter-gatherer ancestors had to work hard for their living. Wirral was no 'leisure peninsula' in that period of history!

The landscape of Mesolithic Wirral, and of England as a whole, was wooded. It developed, by about 7,500 years ago, from fairly open woods of pine, birch and hazel into a denser forest of oak, elm, lime and ash. Where trees died, fell and decayed, small glades encouraged the growth of edible plants including blackberries, barberries, sloes, crab-apples, haws and hazelnuts. Weeds like fat hen, knotgrass, knaw, corn spurry and chickweed could also be eaten. Mammals included deer and auroch (wild cattle, now extinct), elk, wild boar, badgers, hedgehogs, various wild cats and smaller mammals like shrews. The Dee, the Mersey and the sea offered a rich and varied diet from fish and molluscs to seals. Dogs, used for hunting, were the only domesticated animals. There is evidence that Mesolithic groups periodically burned some woodland deliberately to create clearings, probably to provide 'killing grounds' for animals rather than to sow edible plants.

In the south, the English Channel was not formed until about 6500 BCE. For two thousand years before that, the main routes for people moving from the Eurasian landmass were in the east and south of England. These immigrants were all hunter-gatherers following a nomadic lifestyle.

Traditionally, the story of early Britain has been understood as waves of invaders displacing or annihilating the previous inhabitants. Archaeology, however, suggests that this is fundamentally mistaken. For more than ten thousand years people have moved into – and out of – Britain, sometimes in large numbers, sometimes in small groups, but there has always been a basic continuity of population.

The earliest human settlement (it is perhaps an exaggeration to describe it as a village) yet found on Merseyside was located in fields at Greasby. It dates from approximately 7000 BCE and was excavated, between 1987 and 1990, by archaeologists from National Museums on Merseyside.

The site was discovered by archaeologists from National Museums Liverpool, by field walking: prehistoric sites can be identified by the trained eye when worked flint tools

Chert tool

Mesolithic hut

and pottery are brought to the surface by modern deep ploughing. These are the most frequently found and reliable clues, because stone tools are very hard wearing and so are the most likely of human artefacts to survive.

The Greasby site has provided evidence of the mobility of the family, or several families of hunter-gatherers who once lived there. The principal evidence is that nearly all of the stone tools are made of chert, the nearest source of which is on the Welsh side of the River Dee. It is likely, therefore, that these people spent part of the year in North Wales. The sea-level at that time was much lower than it is today, so it would have been easier for them to ford the Dee.

Like flint, chert is a silicate, composed of silicon and oxygen. Both flint and chert are aggregates of microscopic crystals of quartz, found in calcareous sedimentary rocks. Chert, however, is inferior to flint for knapping. It was rarely used for making cutting tools, though flake knives are found occasionally. Large pieces of chert were often used instead of flint to form scrapers and piercing tools. It was frequently used – as it was at Greasby – as an alternative to flint for microliths (arrowheads). In the British Isles, flint occurs in chalk, and chert occurs in carboniferous limestone. The area nearest to Greasby from which chert can be obtained is the band of carboniferous limestone that lies immediately south of the millstone grit hills which run parallel to the River Dee on the Welsh side.

What the archaeologists discovered at Greasby was a hearth or fireplace, and a number of pits, which may initially have been used for storing food but had later been filled with rubbish. Some burnt hazelnuts were found in the vicinity of the hearth. At the bottom of one pit, hidden under a layer of pebbles, they found a collection of roughly shaped pieces of flint, ready to be worked into arrowheads. There were various stone tools that could have been used for preparing food, working bone or wood, or for hunting. A small area in which flakes of flint were found was probably where a specialist flint knapper made spear- and arrow-heads for hunting and scrapers for removing hair and skin from prey. The group's shelters would probably have resembled 'benders' made of animal skins stretched over a framework of pliable branches. All the evidence suggested that the group may have sometimes stayed at the site for months at a time.

There are probably a number of such sites on the low sandstone ridge in Greasby, but this is the only one that has been excavated. Palaeolithic hunter-gatherer groups may well have returned frequently to this same area over hundreds of years. A few miles away, at Thurstaston, an even denser concentration of stone tools has been found, representing another important site of the period.

The site at Greasby – and possibly the one at Thurstaston – was probably a base camp: the group would have had a number of less elaborate camps around Wirral and in North Wales that would have been used overnight by hunters, and for killing and butchering animals.

Throughout prehistory there was a large variety and number of small-scale societies, and many minor 'tribal' identities, typically lasting perhaps no more than a few generations before splitting, merging or being wiped out. The group that lived for part of each year at the Greasby site was just one of many. These groups would have been in contact – and sometimes in conflict – with their neighbours, and sometimes with more distant groups, as evidenced by finds of imported objects.

The period from the arrival of the earliest modern humans to the beginning of recorded history is about ten thousand years, or four hundred generations. Yet we know very little about what went on through this long span of time; it is hard even to answer in detail the question, 'Who were the early inhabitants of Wirral?', because they have left no accounts of themselves. We know nothing of family or individual names, nor can we be sure what language they spoke. We can speculate that the men were bearded, as they had no blades sharp enough to make shaving possible, and that men and women wore clothes made of animal skins.

All we have for certain are the clues found in the scattered remains of their temporary habitations, like those at Greasby. In comparison with the Roman or Norse presence on Wirral, our Mesolithic forebears are likely to keep many of their secrets until the end of time.

♦

3.

A TOWER MORE ELEGANT
THAN BLACKPOOL'S

What was to become the resort of New Brighton was a virtually uninhabited area, known as Rock Point, until 1830 when a retired Liverpool merchant and builder, James Atherton, purchased 170 acres (68.8 hectares) of sand hills and heath land there. The land included a beautiful beach and had views out over Liverpool Bay and across the Mersey to Liverpool itself. It was Atherton's ambition to develop the land as a desirable residential and watering place that would attract the gentry.

Consciously modelled on Brighton in Sussex, it became known as "the new Brighton" and by 1860 it was well established. The resort had wide streets, fashionable villas, handsome hotels and theatres and a pier for steam ferries. The increasing popularity of trains, coupled with frequent ferries to and from Liverpool, began to attract mill workers from Lancashire and large numbers of visitors from Liverpool; after all, why go to Blackpool on the Fylde when New Brighton was on the doorstep? Some day trippers liked the place so much that, when opportunity offered, they jumped at the chance to live in the town all year round and it soon became a highly populated area.

New Brighton's popularity with holiday makers continued into the 20th Century. Towards the end of his life, one local man recalled, "It was a different world then. People used to pour off the ferries in swarms." Even as late as 1953, over the three days of the August Bank Holiday it was calculated that the resort was packed with more than 222,000 visitors. When foreign holidays were beyond the wildest dreams of all but the rich, New Brighton was one of the country's most popular destinations. It boasted miles of sandy beaches, theatres with top class entertainment, a fun fair and Britain's largest and finest outdoor swimming pool. The rivalry with Blackpool was already well established, but it intensified when, inspired by the Eiffel Tower in Paris, Blackpool opened its Tower to the public on 14th May 1894. It had barely opened for business when work began on New Brighton's own tower, designed by the same architects, Maxwell & Tuke of Manchester.

The Tower was financed by The New Brighton Tower and Recreation Company Limited, which purchased the Rock Point Estate, an area of more than 20 acres (8 hectares). As planned, the tower was to be 544 feet (165.8 m) high, with an assembly hall, winter gardens, refreshment rooms and a cycle track. It was emphasised by the Tower and Recreation Company that its tower would be more elegant than Blackpool's.

The foundation stone of the building at the base of the tower was laid on 22nd June 1896. The builders were Handysides & Company of Derby, and the tower itself consumed more than a thousand tons (907.1 tonnes) of mild steel. Crucially for local pride, as built it was 567 feet 6 inches (173 m) to the top of the flagstaff at the summit and its height above sea level was 621 feet (189.2 m). At the time it was the tallest structure in the entire country, and it could be seen for miles around: Blackpool Tower, in comparison, was a mere 515 feet high (157 m)! It has to be said also that, with its main structural elements of eight tapering vertical members, braced by seven steel rings, it was altogether lighter in appearance than its rival at Blackpool and, as intended, it was undoubtedly more elegant. Four lifts took sightseers to the top of the tower for 6d (2.5p) a head: from there it was possible, on a clear day, to see the Isle of Man, the Lake District and the mountains of Snowdonia. In its first year of opening the tower attracted half a million visitors.

The Tower Ballroom, decorated in white and gold, was one of the largest in the world, with a sprung dance floor on which well over a thousand couples could dance without overcrowding. The stage was large enough to accommodate an orchestra of eighty players. There was a balcony with seats for those who preferred to watch the dancers, behind which was an open space where couples could learn to dance without getting under the feet of the experts. There was also a billiard saloon with five tables. Above the ballroom in the Elevator Hall were a Monkey House and Aviary and a shooting gallery.

With the acquisition of more land and aiming for a degree of sophistication, the Tower Gardens eventually covered about 35 acres (14.1 hectares) in all. A Japanese Tea Room overlooked an ornamental lake where a real gondolier would take sweethearts gliding over the water in a Venetian gondola, and in the Parisian Tea Garden (laid out in the style of the Tuilleries in Paris) you could have a cup of tea while watching a Pierrot troupe perform.

Elsewhere in the gardens was a fairground, a theatre, an athletics stadium with a cycle track, and a roller-skating rink. A Wild West show staged in 1908 was so popular that ticket touts made a killing. It is said that the cowboys

New Brighton Tower from sea

New Brighton beach 1905

caused mayhem with their lassos when out on the town on their evenings off, while local landlords were ordered by the Council to refrain from selling intoxicating liquor to the 'Red Indians'.

Towards the river end of the gardens, there was an outdoor dance floor which held five hundred couples where, starting at 9 o'clock in the morning at the height of the season, a Military Band played. Above the dance floor there was a high wire for tightrope walking, which was not provided with a safety net. The tightrope walker, James Hardy, once bet another man that he could walk across the high wire carrying a girl. He won the bet, too, when he carried the barmaid from the Ferry Hotel across on his shoulders – presumably not while there were any dancers on the floor below!

With so many attractions and enormous numbers of visitors, it was no wonder that the Tower grounds needed a private Police force of fifteen men to patrol around and keep order.

On the outbreak of the Great War members of the public were no longer allowed to go up to the top of the Tower "for reasons of security". During the war years the steel structure of the Tower became rusty and neglected and, once hostilities ceased, the cost of renovation was more than the New Brighton Tower Company could afford. The dismantling of the Tower began on 7th May 1919 and was completed in June 1921. The Ballroom and Theatre were retained and remained open.

After the Second World War, (during which the basement was used as an air raid shelter), the Ballroom played host first to crooners, then to skiffle bands and, when the '60s dawned to the 'Merseybeat'. The Beatles appeared there on twenty-seven separate occasions; their last performance taking place on Friday 14th June 1963 when they were supported by Gerry and the Pacemakers and five other bands. After that the sparkle seemed to grow dull; the buildings began to look seedy and down at heel. Perhaps mercifully, in 1969 a fire destroyed most of what remained and Blackpool's only serious rival was no more.

Today New Brighton is a rather quieter place. On a sunny morning it's somewhere for people to go jogging, cycling or walking the dog along the wide, almost deserted promenade, past small groups of eternally patient sea anglers. New Brighton has been through the worst in the '70s and '80s, and it is looking clean and tidy as it waits for a new regeneration plan that will finally bring the long promised investment needed to realise its potential anew.

◆

4.

THE FORTS OF LIVERPOOL BAY

If you look out over Liverpool Bay, either from the north Wirral coast or anywhere from north Liverpool to Formby, on a clear day you will see a horizon crowded with offshore wind generators as well as a gas production platform. Remarkably few people know, however, that during the Second World War you would have seen some quite different structures out there which, in engineering terms, were their direct ancestors. These were the spidery, ungainly-looking anti-aircraft forts built as part of Britain's defences against the Luftwaffe.

Probably the best known of these were the forts off the coasts of Kent, Essex and Suffolk, officially called the 'Thames Estuary Special Defence Units', although they were later given the code name "Uncle" for security reasons. More commonly they were known to the military simply as 'Maunsell Forts', named after their designer. In fact, because they were built in secrecy, it was not until the 1960s, when a number of the forts in the Thames estuary were used as 'pirate' radio stations that most members of the public knew of them. Even today, few people know that the first of Maunsell's 'army' forts – more elaborate than his earlier 'naval' forts – were sited not in the Thames Estuary but in Liverpool Bay.

Guy Anson Maunsell (1884–1961) was a civil engineer of great vision and energy, who became a designer of real genius. He served in France as an officer in the Royal Engineers in 1917. The following year he was seconded to design and construct a shipyard at Shoreham in Essex to build concrete sea-going vessels. After the Great War he worked with Sir Alexander Gibb, the chief engineer at the Ministry of Transport, designing a barrage and combined road- and railway-bridge for the River Severn that included a tidal power scheme; the barrage was never built, although the plans have had the dust blown off them several times since.

As war with Nazi Germany became inevitable, Maunsell sent numerous design proposals to the Admiralty. In October 1940 the War Office instructed him to design a sea fort, which could be towed into coastal waters and grounded on the sea bed, to defend the coast from an enemy attack either by sea or air. In today's terms, the units he designed would have cost something like £1.5m and no action was taken. However, a year later with German bombing intensifying Maunsell's idea was revived. A 'naval' fort was sited in the Thames estuary, comprising four towers each weighing about 4,500 tons. They were built of reinforced concrete at Northfleet then towed out and sunk on site in 1942.

Proposals to construct forts in the Humber Estuary never materialised, but it was decided that, if at all possible, some should be sited in Liverpool Bay because of the Mersey's crucial role in receiving convoys of merchant ships from the United States. In the ever-shifting seabed conditions of Liverpool Bay it required all Maunsell's ingenuity and skill to ground the forts in about 40 feet (12.1 m) of water with a tide range of approximately 20 feet (6 m). After a series of experiments, he designed a foundation that would bury itself in the sand and, having done so, would then offer very little obstruction to the tidal currents or movement of the waves.

Above:
Maunsell Forts being built at
Bromborough

Left:
Maunsell Forts in
Liverpool Bay

There were three Mersey forts, named 'Formby', 'Queens' and 'Burbo' after the sandbanks on which they were sited. Each was, in effect, a maritime version of the standard land-based anti-aircraft (or 'ack-ack') battery. The forts consisted of four towers each mounting 3.7 inch heavy ack-ack guns and two towers armed with 40mm Bofors guns and a searchlight platform, all controlled centrally. The guns had to be spaced about 100 feet apart, which dictated that there should be seven separate towers, connected by walkways high above the waves. Equipped with radar prediction equipment, the forts were the first line of defence against enemy aircraft, submarines or ships coming in from the sea.

The Mersey forts were taller than those built later in the Thames Estuary, to take account of the deeper water in which they were sited. They were built by the Cleveland Bridge and Engineering Company on a site at Bromborough, and were positioned in Liverpool Bay in the first half of 1942. The Thames 'army' forts were commenced in August 1942 and the final tower was not completed until June 1943.

These were massive structures which had to be fully operational even in the worst wind and sea conditions. The hollow cylindrical, reinforced concrete legs of the towers were 65 feet (19.8 m) high, with an external diameter of 3 feet (0.91 m). Each leg was pre-cast in three separate sections, each weighing 5 tons (4.5 tonnes) and 17 feet (5.18 m) in length. A concrete cap at the top of each leg, with two embedded rolled steel joists formed the base for the steel superstructure. An octagonal steel unit, with a bottom, intermediate and top deck, formed the superstructure of the tower. The width between each pair of parallel walls was 36 feet (10.97 m), the walls being made of ¼ inch (0.63 cm) steel plate. Armoured parapets were provided around the top deck and armour plate around the magazine chambers where ammunition was stored. Five of the seven towers that formed each fort had mooring facilities so that they could be re-supplied by ship under all but the worst of sea conditions. Electric hoists were provided to unload cargo. In 1941, when ferry services across the River Mersey were suspended because of the danger of mines, the ferry boat "Upton" was requisitioned for use as a supply vessel for the forts.

The exterior steelwork of the accommodation units, each of which weighed 1000 tons (907 tonnes), was protected from the weather by three coats of bituminous paint, the top coat of which was camouflage. Steel framed windows, specially designed and made by Critall, incorporating blackout shutters and louvres, provided daylight and ventilation. Every tower had a central heating installation and a boiler to supply hot fresh water and provided sleeping accommodation and recreational rooms for some of the officers and men. Each fort complex was manned by between 165 and 265 officers and men.

The walls of the accommodation were insulated, and floors had a ¾ inch (1.9 cm) covering of asphalt. The floor of the top deck was armour-plated. The mess area for the men was in the Bofors gun tower while the officers' quarters and mess were in the central control tower. The searchlight tower was equipped with three 30 kw diesel powered generators which provided the electrical power for the whole fort.

After playing a vital part in the defence of Merseyside, although there is no evidence that they ever saw action,

WIRRAL CAMERA OBSCURA   ANDY WOOD

one fort was badly damaged in a storm and not long after the war another was damaged when a ship collided with it. The Liverpool Bay forts were demolished in the early 1950s.

Guy Maunsell made a further significant contribution to the eventual Allied victory. In 1940 he had proposed a floating harbour scheme to Admiral Hughes Hallet. When Winston Churchill suggested the same thing for the D Day landings in Normandy in 1944, it was Maunsell's plans that brought the idea to fruition in the form of the Mulberry harbour. It was possibly the greatest civil engineering achievement of the war. The industrial and economic benefits of the Maunsell Forts are incalculable: they provided the design principles for the oil and gas exploration and production rigs on which so much of the modern world depends.

♦

5.

A MARINERS' FLOATING CHURCH

Liverpool and Birkenhead once had an unlikely connection with the Emperor Napoleon. For more than sixty years the wooden former frigate HMS 'Tees' did service as a Mariners' Church, first at George's Dock in Liverpool and later in the West Float, Birkenhead.

The 'Tees' was built at Bideford in Devonshire and launched in 1817. She was commissioned in 1818 and her first commander was Captain George Rennie. Her maiden voyage was to the island of St Helena where the Emperor Napoleon had been exiled following his defeat at Waterloo and his surrender. Napoleon had hoped that he would be granted asylum in England, but the British Government preferred to confine him to St Helena, which lies in the South Atlantic 1,200 miles (1,931 km) from the coast of Angola. The island, which is approximately 10 miles (16km) long by 7 miles (11.26 km) wide, had been fortified with guard posts and gun emplacements to prevent any attempt to liberate the Emperor. HMS 'Tees' was one of three frigates and two other vessels that were kept on standby as guard ships, while six other vessels were deployed on observation duties with two of their number continually circling the island.

The 'Tees' remained on station at St Helena until Napoleon's death on 5th May 1821. Captain Rennie, however, who must have been something of a martinet, soon had other things to worry about. On 3rd July 1821 he appeared before a court martial at Portsmouth charged with cruelty, oppression and conduct unbecoming an officer towards the crew of the 'Tees'. On 14th July he was acquitted of the charge of cruelty but was found guilty of inflicting irregular punishments on several of the ship's company; for this he was dismissed the service. However, the court drew to the Admiralty's attention the licentiousness, drunkenness and insubordination of the crew, and Rennie was restored to the active list in 1822.

On 6th January 1822 the 'Tees' sailed from Spithead for the East Indies station under the command of Captain Thomas Coe. In July 1824, following the death of the squadron commander, Commodore Charles Grant, Captain Coe hoisted a commander's broad pennant on board the frigate HMS 'Liffey' and carried out the duties of senior officer until he was relieved by Sir James Brisbane who promoted Capt. Frederick Marryatt of HMS 'Larne' to take command of the 'Tees'. On her return to England, after less than ten years service, HMS 'Tees' was paid off at Chatham at the beginning of 1826.

In late spring 1826 she sailed round Land's End and up the Irish Sea to Liverpool, where her masts and rigging were removed and she was converted for use as the Mariners' Church. Entry to the church was by means of a gangplank which led to a doorway that had been cut through the ship's side on the starboard bow. HMS 'Tees' officially opened as a floating church on 17th May 1827. She was moored in a corner of George's Dock, the first enclosed dock to be built on the Mersey, close to Mann Island. Originally known as 'Mersey Island' this was an artificial island between George's Dock and Canning Dock on one side and the River Mersey to the west. It was renamed after John Mann, an oil-stone dealer, who died there in 1784.

It was at her mooring in George's Dock that William Gawin Herdman (1805-82) painted the 'Tees'. No other artist did more to document Liverpool than Herdman. As a boy of thirteen he had begun making notes about how the city and its buildings were changing around him and later, entirely self-taught, he produced dozens of watercolour views of the city at a time when it was experiencing unprecedented economic growth. He quickly built a successful career as a commercial artist and his work continues to be in demand to this day.

The first minister of the Mariners' Church was the Reverend Dr William Scoresby. He was succeeded by the Reverend William Maynard in 1832. Maynard remained in his post for over forty years. The services on the 'Tees' were attended not only by seafarers but also by residents of the city. To begin with attendances were high but by the mid-1850s few seamen were attending. The 'Tees' sank at her mooring in June 1872 when some of her bottom planks rotted through.

It was not quite the end for the ship, however. In 1879 she was taken over by the Mersey Mission to Seamen, made watertight (possibly by lashing tarpaulin tightly around the hull, and towed across the river to a new mooring in the West Float, Birkenhead, (which had been opened in 1860), where she replaced the small existing Mission and Reading Room. Precisely where the 'Tees' was moored is not known. However, given the position of the entrance door on her starboard bow, she would have been moored, as she had been in George's Dock, in a corner. The most likely locations in the West Float where this could be achieved – Canada Creek, Rank's Creek and Gillbrook Basin – all lie on the south side of the Float. Any of them

George's Dock

The Mariner's Church, formerly HMS 'Tees'

would have been suitable, and they are all close to the Graving Docks where the ship could have had permanent repairs made to her hull.

The Mersey Mission had been set up at a meeting on 22nd November 1865. Its aim was to give spiritual guidance and practical help to seafarers whose ships docked on either side of the river. To begin with the Mission was a branch of the Missions to Seamen which had been set up in London by W H G Kingston. In 1873, however, it became independent and was renamed the 'Mersey Mission to Seamen'. In 1859, the Reverend Edward Thring, the Mission's Superintendent Chaplain started a campaign against the dishonest practice known as 'crimping'; men who claimed to be lodging house keepers would board ships as they entered the River Mersey and offer sailors rooms in lodgings that did not exist. The Reverend Thring's campaign sent sailors to respectable lodging houses and helped to stamp out 'crimping'. The Mission continues its work to the present day, based now at Colonsay House in Crosby.

It appears that the 'Tees' finally ceased to be used by the Mission some time in the 1880s or '90s, although the records are few and it is not known where she was broken up, although it is possible that it was on the beach at The Sloyne off New Ferry where, famously, Brunel's 'Great Eastern' was scrapped in 1889. George's Dock in Liverpool, where the 'Tees' was moored for fifty-two years, was later drained and filled in to become the site of the Liver Building.

♦

6.

PIECES OF HISTORY
DOWN THE SLIPWAY

When William Laird moved, with his wife and son, from Greenock on the Clyde to Birkenhead on the Mersey, in 1805, he had no intention of founding a shipbuilding company that would send pieces of history down its slipways for over a hundred and seventy years. In 1824 Laird and a partner, Daniel Horton, established the Birkenhead Iron Works which manufactured boilers. The partnership was dissolved in 1828 and William was joined in business by his son John. It was John who realised that the same techniques used for bending and riveting iron plates to make boilers could also be used to build ships' hulls, and who led the firm to begin its involvement in iron shipbuilding.

The company's first shipbuilding order was of an extremely modest nature; a 60 foot (18.2 m), 60 ton (54.4 tonne) lighter, the "Wye", built in 1829, which was followed by two others in 1832, for the Irish Inland Steam Navigation company, which had its headquarters at Killaloe, Co Clare. The company owned slate quarries, and marble was also described as "an important article of trade". The lighters were probably ordered for the transport of these materials. However, the launch of "Lady Lansdowne" marked the company's real entry into shipbuilding.

The "Lady Lansdowne", the first of a long series of paddle steamers was built in 1833 for the City of Dublin Steam Packet Company, which had begun operating steam ships between Dublin and Liverpool in 1822. Among the many paddles steamers turned out by the yard was "L'Egyptien", built in 1837 for Mehemet Ali, Pasha of Egypt. Mehemet Ali, an ethnic Albanian, had created an empire in the Middle East and profited from the rivalry between Britain and France. The steamer may, in fact, have been a gift from the British government in the endless jockeying with the French for influence over the Pasha.

Not all the paddle steamers were built for shipping companies. The first armed vessel built at the yard was "Ariadne", ordered in 1839 by the Honourable East India Company for the 'Bombay Marine', the Company's private navy. The Marine was intended mainly for coastal protection, but it operated from the Persian Gulf to the Indian Ocean and in time of war its ships worked alongside the Royal Navy. "Ariadne" was followed, in 1840, by three gunboats, "Soudan", "Albert" and "Wilberforce", for the Royal Navy itself. In 1842 the "Guadalupe", a paddle frigate was built for the Mexican Government.

Paddle-driven ships represented the cutting edge of naval architecture until 1852 when the Weaver Navigation Company ordered "Weaver", the first screw driven ship to be built by Laird's. Thereafter, the Birkenhead yard was regarded as the finest in the world and orders poured in from as far away as the USA, Russia, Brazil, Australia, Peru, China, Nigeria, Ceylon, and Japan.

No doubt intended for service in the Crimea, fifteen wooden gunboats and fifteen mortar boats were built in 1855-56 for the Royal Navy, although the Crimean War came to an end in February 1856.

In 1858 the paddle steamer "Ma Robert" was built for Dr Livingstone's government sponsored Zambezi Expedition. The vessel was paid for by MacGregor Laird, a Scottish philanthropist. The name "Ma Robert" was given to it, under an old Scots custom, to honour Livingstone's wife, Mary, mother of their first-born son, Robert.

On the other side of the Atlantic, in 1861, eleven states seceded from the USA and formed the Confederate States of America. With civil war inevitable, Laird's was secretly commissioned to build an armed vessel for the Confederacy in 1862. The 1050 ton (952.5 tonne) screw-driven ship, given the number V0290 by the yard, was launched as the "Enrica", but was then fitted out as an armed cruiser and commissioned on 24th August 1862 as CSS "Alabama". After sinking or capturing numerous Union ships, she was brought to battle by the USS "Kearsarge" off Cherbourg on 19th June 1864. In little more than an hour from the first shot being fired, "Alabama" was reduced to a sinking wreck and surrendered.

By the late 1860s technology had advanced again and Laird's was building ships with twin screws. The Royal Dutch Navy ordered two twin screw ironclads "De Steir" and "Heligerlee" which were launched in 1868, and the following year HMS "Vanguard", a twin screw battleship was built for the Royal Navy.

We should not overlook the human element in the stories of the vessels Laird's sent out over the oceans. "Britannia" a screw driven cable ship, was built in 1885 for the Cable & Wireless Company. Her career was on the whole one of hard work and little excitement, However, R C Marsh, the Bosun's Mate on the "Britannia" was awarded the Royal

Humane Society's Bronze Medal for an act of bravery. At 5.00 pm on the 20th March 1911 a seaman, James Stevens, accidentally fell from a boat in the harbour at St. Helena. The Bosun's Mate, despite having his right hand bandaged as the result of an accident, jumped in and succeeded in saving him.

"Almirante Lynch" and "Almirante Condell", for the Chilean Government in 1890, were the first gunboats armed with torpedoes to be built by Laird's. The first successful attack using a torpedo took place during the Chilean Civil War when the two Birkenhead built torpedo boats attacked the ironclad "Blanco Encalada" on the night of April 23rd 1891. The "Almirante Condell" fired three Whitehead torpedoes at the ironclad but they all missed. The "Almirante Lynch" then fired another salvo of three weapons one of which hit and blew a hole 15 ft by 7 ft (4.5 by 2.1 m) below the waterline. The "Blanco Encalada" sank immediately with the loss of 180 officers and men. One result of the explosion was that the ironclad's Captain, Don Luis Goni, survived and was seen swimming ashore with one arm around the ship's mascot, a tame llama. The animal was later taken as mascot on board HMS "Warspite", the Flagship of the Royal Navy's Pacific Station, until it disgraced itself by eating the epaulettes of an Admiral's dress uniform, after which it was sent to London Zoo!

Once torpedo boats had proved to be effective, a new type of naval vessel was needed to counteract them. Laird's yard built HMS "Lynx", the first 'torpedo boat destroyer' in 1894, after which thirty-five destroyers were built up to 1907.

In the same period steam powered private yachts were also in demand. Those built in Birkenhead included "More

Vane" for the Duke of Westminster, "Princess Alice" for the Prince of Monaco and "Valiant" for William Kissam Vanderbilt, the American railroad millionaire (who also became the holder of the World Land Speed Record of 92.30 mph (148.5 kph) in a Mercedes in 1904).

Not all the vessels built by Laird's were destined for far off places. In 1908, for example, the yard turned out the "Leviathan", an impressively large dredger for the Mersey Docks and Harbour Board. In 1910 it also built "Snaefell" for the Isle of Man Steam Packet Company, (all of the company's ferries over the years were built in Birkenhead). But, as the balance of power in Europe tilted towards war, Laird's would soon be called on to devote all its resources to building warships for the Royal Navy.

Before Great Britain entered the Great War on 4th August 1914 she had been engaged in a race with Germany to build fast and heavily armoured ships since the launch of HMS "Dreadnought" in 1905. The "Queen Elizabeth" class of 'super dreadnoughts' marked the climax of this race. Mounting eight 15 inch guns, the ships of the class were the first oil-fired British battleships, capable of a speed of 23 knots. They possessed an almost perfect combination of gun power, armour protection and speed.

These ships, however, were built at Devonport and at Govan on the Clyde. Laird's was fully occupied building cruisers and large numbers of submarines and destroyers. In 1915 the yard built the light cruisers "Birkenhead" and "Chester", ordered for Greece but taken over by the British Government, both of which took part in the Battle of Jutland; the destroyers "Gabriel", "Abdiel" and "Kempenfelt"; the light cruisers "Castor" and "Constance", and two E Class submarines. 1916 saw the launch of

The sinking of CSS 'Alabama' by the USS 'Kearsage'

'Tynwald' approaching the Liverpool Landing Stage

six destroyers, "Ithuriel", "Parker", "Grenville", "Hoste", "Seymour" and "Saumarez"; two more E Class submarines and the light cruiser "Caledon". In 1917, as well as two L Class submarines and three destroyers, the yard resumed the building of merchant ships with "Oropasa" for the Pacific Steam Navigation Company. By 1918 only two flotilla leaders, "Campbell" and "Mackay" were built for the Navy and two H Class submarines as well as the light cruiser "Cairo". Although construction of two more L Class submarines had begun they were broken up and an order for a further six was cancelled.

In the inter-war years Laird's resumed the building of cargo ships and passenger liners both for British and foreign clients. "La Playa" built in 1923 for the United Fruit Company was the first of many refrigerated dry cargo vessels for lines like Elders & Fyffes. Laird's built a wide variety of vessels and other marine structures including liquid latex carriers, tugs, pontoons, dredgers, shipping beacons, lake steamers, colliers, pilot vessels, ferries and oil tankers.

In the immediate post-war years no warships were built, but on 17th December 1925 the battleship HMS "Rodney" was launched. After fitting out she was commissioned into the Royal Navy on the 7th December 1927. She was the largest warship yet built in Birkenhead, with a displacement of 33,900 tons (30,753 tonnes). Her armament was nine 16 inch guns in three triple turrets; twelve 6 inch guns in pairs. To fight off attack from the air, she carried six 4.7 inch anti-aircraft guns in singles, twenty-four 2 pounder AA guns and twelve machine guns. She also mounted two torpedo tubes and carried two seaplanes, which were launched by catapults mounted amidships, and recovered by crane. "Rodney" needed a complement of 1,330 to 1,558 men, had a maximum speed of 23 knots and a range of 7,000 miles (11,265 km). She was to serve with the home Fleet for most of World War II, but was detached to join Force H in 1943 for service in the Mediterranean. Her most celebrated action was the part she played in the sinking of the "Bismarck" on the 27th May 1941.

Perhaps the best known vessel to be built for the Royal Navy in this period was the aircraft carrier "Ark Royal", not least because of the iconic photograph taken by the Liverpool photographer E Chambré Hardman. The third ship to carry the name, she displaced 22,000 tons (19,958 tonnes) and was launched in 1937. She too would take part in the hunt for the "Bismarck", but she was torpedoed and sunk by a German U-Boat in November 1941.

Launched on 3rd May 1939, the battleship HMS "Prince of Wales" also saw action against the "Bismarck" but was not in at the kill, having been damaged in an earlier encounter with her and the "Prins Eugen". She was at Singapore in October 1941, but was sunk off Malaya (along with HMS Repulse) by Japanese torpedo bombers on the 10th December that year, despite mounting forty-eight 2 pounder anti-aircraft guns.

One of the most tragic incidents involving a Laird's built vessel was played out less than forty miles (64 km) from where it was built. HMS "Thetis", a T Class submarine, was launched in 1938. During her maiden voyage on 1st June 1939, carrying 103 people including 34 engineers from the yard, her nose buried itself in the river bed with her stern above water. A major rescue operation was mounted and for three days the men on board fought against the effects of carbon dioxide poisoning, waiting for a rescue which never came; only four men escaped. Eventually "Thetis" was salvaged and, such was the Navy's need for submarines, she was not scrapped but gutted, refitted, re-equipped, and renamed HMS "Thunderbolt". But there was to be no happy ending: exactly a year and a day after the fatal accident she was lost in a depth charge attack in the Mediterranean. Incredibly, history repeated itself and she sank bow down and stern up in the air. There were no survivors.

Large numbers of submarines, escort vessels, landing craft, destroyers and sloops were built during the war, reaching a peak in 1943-44. Cargo vessels continued to be built for the Blue Star Line, Holts, Shaw-Savill and others, to replace merchant shipping lost to the U-boat packs.

After the war the yard began to produce increasing numbers of oil tankers for companies like Shell, Esso and Burmah as well as for foreign companies. In 1951 a tanker for Yacimeientos Petroliferos Fiscales of Argentina was to have been called "Eva Peron" but the wife of the President of Argentina died on 26th July 1952 and the ship was subsequently renamed "Fray Luis Beltran".

"Manxman" was another of the many Irish Sea ferries, beginning with the "Manx Fairy" paddle steamer in 1853, built over the years for the Isle of Man Steam Packet Company. "Manxman" was launched from Cammell Laird's on 8th February 1955 and her trials took place on the Clyde on the 12th May when she reached a speed of 21.95 knots. She operated the route between Liverpool and Douglas from when she was built until 1982. Currently she is on the National Register of Historic Ships and awaiting restoration.

As it had from the beginning, what was now Cammell Laird's continued to produced all kinds of vessels, civil and military; chemical tankers, vehicle ferries, ammonia carriers, refrigerated cargo ships and cable layers among them. The yard's first container ship "Canadian Pacific Trader" was built in 1970.

HMS "Birmingham" and HMS "Coventry", both Type 42 guided missile destroyers, were launched in 1973 and 1974 respectively. When they were built it was in the expectation that if they should ever fire missiles in anger it would most likely be in a conflict with the Warsaw Pact countries. Nobody had even considered the possibility that they might go to war against Argentina. "Coventry", however, was part of the task force that set sail from Portsmouth at the beginning of April 1982. On 25th May Argentine aircraft attacked HMS "Coventry" and the frigate "Broadsword". Three bombs hit the "Coventry", tearing out a large part of her port side. A fierce fire took hold immediately and water began pouring into the ship. The order to abandon ship was given and within twenty minutes HMS "Coventry" capsized with the loss of twenty lives.

In 1983 the shipyard was dominated by the growing bulk of the semi-submersible oil exploration rig "Sovereign Explorer", the first such structure to be built on Merseyside. After its launch, the rig was usually to be found in foreign waters, but it became headline news in this country in 2000, when four Greenpeace volunteers occupied the rig in the Cromarty Firth, Scotland, as part of a campaign to protest about climate change and to protect marine life in the north east Atlantic.

Though no-one in Birkenhead could quite believe it, the conventionally powered attack submarine HMS "Unicorn", built in 1992, was to be the last ship to carry the maker's plate of Cammell Laird. Worse still, she was not to remain in service for very long. On October 16th 1994 "Unicorn" carried out the very last dive by a British diesel electric submarine with the Flag Officer Submarines, Vice Admiral Roger Lane-Nott, aboard. The vessel was paid off the following year after only 478 days in commission. Admiral Sir Hugo White, the Commander-in-Chief Fleet signalled, "As the flotilla now moves into the all-nuclear age, HMS "Unicorn" has in her short commission upheld to the very end the finest traditions of her forebears". Much the same could be said of the shipyard workers who themselves were paid off soon after the submarine left the slipway.

The doors of the shipyard closed in 1993 for what many people assumed was the last time, the business having been sunk by declining orders from the Ministry of Defence and its ineligibility for subsidies for building merchant ships. Like the final flicker of a dying fire, part of the yard is operated by the Coastline Group, not to build but to repair and refit ships. It is unlikely that shipbuilding will ever return to the Mersey: a great and nationally important tradition is at an end.

In 2004, Paranormal.Science, a group based on Wirral was contacted by members of staff working in an office building on the former Cammell Laird site, following a series of unusual experiences. These included apparitions, cold spots and sense-of-presence experiences in a ground floor corridor area. Paranormal Science says, "The shipyard... was a major source of employment and built many famous boats and ships. It is estimated that more than 350,000 men and women worked at this shipyard over the years... perhaps some of them remain?"

♦

7.

WIRRAL FORTIFICATIONS

One thing that Wirral conspicuously lacks is a castle, but it isn't entirely without fortifications, the best known of which is Fort Perch Rock at New Brighton. However, it is not the only structure built for defence purposes: scattered about the peninsula are at least eight 'pillboxes' built during the Second Word War.

'Pillboxes' are small structures, usually of reinforced concrete, which were designed to defend areas and sites that would be vulnerable to attack in the event of an invasion. Depending on the type and location, they were intended to be manned by anything from one to ten men armed with rifles, light or heavy machine guns or small anti-tank weapons.

The pillbox had been developed during the intense static trench warfare of the Western Front in the Great War, where they gave a great advantage over enemy troops attacking over open ground. In the Second World War they were deployed in the UK on the coast and on canals, rivers and railway lines. Built by local construction firms to a number of standard designs – which could be modified to suit a particular site – many still remain. They were sited to defend road junctions, river crossings and other strategic sites, and when built in groups, were sited so as to give each other covering fire.

Many pillboxes were disguised in some way, or incorporated in existing buildings like barns, bridges, houses or even pubs. One of the most unusual was built as an extension of, and designed to match the Great Hall at Merchant Taylor's School, near Rickmansworth, Hertfordshire. This particular pillbox formed part of London's outer ring of anti-invasion defences..

Following the evacuation of British forces from Dunkirk in 1940 the War Office feared a German invasion. Defences, known as 'Stoplines', were hurriedly devised, consisting of obstacles and fortifications located to take advantage of the natural lie of the land. The basic concept was laid out in a Southern Command memo dated 22nd June 1940 which stated:

"The immediate object is to divide England into several small fields surrounded by a hedge of anti-tank obstacles which is strong defensively, using natural accidents of the ground where possible. Should Armoured Fighting Vehicles attack or airborne attacks break into the enclosures, the policy will be to close the gate by blocking the crossing over the obstacles and to let the dogs - in the shape of armoured formations or other troops – round up the cattle." (Whoever wrote the memo should be congratulated for sustaining his agricultural metaphor at such length!)

Clearly, the Stoplines were intended to block the progress of German armoured columns and set them up for a counter-attack by defending forces. A Stopline would consist of continuous anti-tank obstacles, natural if possible, covered by pillboxes and other prepared positions.

It is hard to avoid the feeling that the Stoplines plan was conceived in haste, if not panic. Admittedly, there wasn't

Above:
Type 22 pillbox,
Bromborough,
Pool

Left:
Entrance to a pillbox

a great deal of previous planning to draw on. Defensive tactics had not been studied in any great detail in the inter-war years, which is remarkable given the success of German field defences during the Great War, which were based on deep defensive zones and counter-attack units.

The threat the Stoplines were intended to neutralise was that of tanks but, although a Stopline could have halted a column of light tanks or armoured cars advancing without reconnaissance or air cover, the German army would never have used unsupported light armour. The Panzer divisions included infantry, artillery and engineer units as well as heavy tanks. It should have been obvious, from German tactics in Belgium, France and Russia, that the Panzers would brush aside defences like the Stoplines.

The original Stopline plan seems not to have been sufficiently thought through, not least because it was unrealistic about the sort of threat it would confront. On another level, however, it may have seemed that there was no alternative. Any form of defence in depth requires sufficient forces to mount a counter-attack. In the months immediately following Dunkirk such forces simply did not exist, particularly as the formations plucked from the beaches had had to abandon all their equipment. But as the months passed without an invasion, and the army was re-equipped, the original Stoplines doctrine was abandoned.

By far the greater numbers of these defences were constructed in eastern and southern England, since any German invasion would have had to take place there. However, in Scotland, north-west England, in Cardigan Bay and on the Welsh side of the Severn Estuary, considerable stretches of coastline were covered by fixed defences. In addition, all over the country strategic objectives such as docks, factories and transport routes were provided with prepared defensive positions. The remaining examples of pillboxes on Wirral certainly fall into this category.

At Hooton, for instance, a large lozenge-shaped pillbox (a variant of the 'Type 26' standard design) is situated near the site of the former RAF fighter station at Hooton Park, which is now largely occupied by the Vauxhall car plant. It was obviously built as part of the airfield's defences. It has two loop-holes on the front face, now blocked up, and the rear entrance is protected by a blast wall, now covered with ivy. Unusually, two of the loop-holes are in the corners pointing south and west.

On Bromborough Road, not far from Spital Dam, behind the Unilever factory, a Type 22 pillbox provides defensive cover for the road leading to Port Sunlight. The bridge by which the A41 crosses Bromborough Pool is still guarded by pillboxes; on both the east and west sides two Type 24 pillboxes cover the southern approach.

Further to the west, another Type 22 pillbox covers Brimstage Road (B5137) between the M53 roundabout (Jct 4) and Brimstage village.

At Neston a Type 22 covers the B5134 road from the coast as well as the course of the Wirral Way which, at the time of the pillbox's construction, was the railway line from Hooton to West Kirby.

Finally, at West Kirby a now sealed-up Type 22 still stands guard on the B5140 from the coast.

The 'Defence of Britain Project', co-ordinated by the Council for British Archaeology, which ran from 1995 to 2002, produced a national database of surviving defences. Archaeologists working for the English Heritage Monuments Protection Programme are now visiting sites and making recommendations about scheduling them for preservation.

Far more modest than the great castles of Wales, less imposing even than the defensive towers constructed in the south in anticipation of an invasion by Napoleon, even so Wirral's own reminders of the Second World War should be preserved.

♦

8.

FROM SAXON THANES
TO VAUXHALL MOTORS

The name Hooton goes back to pre-Conquest times. It derives from two Saxon words 'ho', meaning a heel or point of land stretching out into a plain or the sea, and 'tun', meaning a farm. The name 'Hotone' appears in the Domesday Book and the manor of Hooton dates from Norman times, when the lands were confiscated from the Saxon thane and granted to Adam de Aldithley by William I. The manor subsequently passed through various hands until 1310, when William de Stanley acquired it by marriage, along with the office of Master Forester of Wirral.

Hooton was to remain the seat of the Earls of Stanley, the senior line of the Earldom of Derby, for 500 years. Towards the end of the 15th Century, they replaced the original hall with a half-timbered Manor House. This, in turn, was succeeded in the early 19th Century by a Palladian mansion of Storeton stone, designed by the architect Samuel Wyatt (1737-1807) for the 5th Baronet, Sir William Stanley. (Wyatt also built Trinity House in London, and the grand portico at Shugborough Hall in Staffordshire.)

The Stanleys occupied Wyatt's imposing Hall for little more than seventy years. Like not a few members of the aristocracy, Sir Thomas Stanley, the 6th Baronet, ran up enormous gambling debts, added to which he had the estate landscaped by the garden designer Humphrey Repton, an unnecessary extravagance in the circumstances. Sir Thomas's banker, Richard Christopher

Naylor of Liverpool, who had grown rich in the cotton trade, bought the estate for £82,000.

Naylor spent a further £52,500 refurbishing the house and building a racecourse, polo ground and heronry in the park. The first race meeting took place on Monday 22nd May 1899 but by then Naylor was living at Kelmarsh Hall, another of his estates, in Northamptonshire. Until the outbreak of the Great War crowds came to enjoy the principal races, 'The Hooton Park Hurdle' and the 'Great Cheshire Chase'. The last meeting was on 17th April 1914, ten days after the declaration of war.

Hooton Hall and park were requisitioned by the Army; a barracks was built and the Hall became a military hospital. The 18th Battalion, King's Liverpool Rifles were stationed at Hooton until they went to the Western Front in 1916. The following year the park became an airfield used by the Royal Flying Corps (RFC) to train pilots from Canada and the USA on the Sopwith Pup. (Some of the airfield buildings survive from this period, including three Grade II* listed 'Belfast Truss' aircraft hangars.) The RFC, which had become the Royal Air Force towards the end of the war, relinquished the site in 1919.

The Hall itself fell into disrepair and was demolished in 1922. If you want to see what remains of Hooton Hall, you must travel to the Llyn peninsula in North Wales. Eight of the massive Ionic columns from the Colonnade of the Hall were rescued in the 1930s by Clough Williams Ellis, the architect of the playful Italianate village of Portmerion, near Porthmadog. Williams Ellis confessed, "For nearly thirty years I forgot all about this rather rash and extravagant purchase until I had my 'Gloriette' idea, by which time these bits and pieces could nowhere be found. Ultimately they were tracked down and dug up from under a garden that had been made on top of them!" (The Gloriette is one of the architect's many visual jokes: the main street of Portmerion winds round The Piazza, from which it is screened by a wall, and then the narrow north doorway of the Gloriette tempts the visitor to explore, and he suddenly finds himself on a balcony overlooking the village.)

In 1927 Hooton Park was purchased, by Liverpool City Council, to serve as an airport for Liverpool and the North West. It became Liverpool Airport officially in 1930, although it was only three years before Liverpool thought again and opened a new airport at Speke. Despite that, however, Hooton remained a flourishing centre for aviation for the next two decades.

In 1929, an aero club was formed, which grew over the next few years to be the most active flying club in Great Britain outside London. It was a national centre for light aircraft, at a time when flying was growing in popularity. The club held local air races, and Hooton Park was a staging post for the King's Cup national air races of the 1930s. Aircraft and aero engines were also manufactured at Hooton (see 'A Fighter in Miniature).

Sir Alan Cobham's Flying Circus, which drew large crowds in the early 1930s, visited Hooton and the 'wing walker' Martin Hearn and other stars of the show performed breathtaking stunts while their planes were in flight. The celebrated aviator Amy Johnson visited the airfield. Ford tri-motor passenger aircraft were also imported from the USA and assembled at Hooton.

Hooton Hall

Margaret Beavan, Mayor of Liverpool (second from right)
at the opening of Liverpool Airport, Hooton Park, 1930

On 10th February 1936, 610 (County of Chester) Squadron, Auxiliary Air Force, was formed at Hooton as a light bomber squadron, equipped with Avro Tutors and Hawker Harts and Hinds. The Tutor looked very similar to the aircraft of the Great War, although it had only entered service in 1930. The Hawkers were more sophisticated and powerful, but they were also biplanes. Even as they were entering service, German engineers were designing monoplane aircraft that would easily outperform the Hart and the Hind.

On 1st January 1939, 610 Squadron was re-equipped as a fighter unit although it retained its Hawker biplanes until the outbreak of war, when it received Fairey Battles and later Hurricanes and, later still, the incomparable Spitfire. All civil flying ceased, and the eighteen light aircraft at the airfield were immobilised and stored under the grandstand of the former racecourse. In June 1940 they were all destroyed in an accidental fire.

During much of World War II Coastal Command operated anti-submarine patrols from RAF Hooton Park. The airfield also had an important role in assembling and repairing aircraft. Martin Hearn Ltd, founded at Hooton in the mid 1930s, assembled or repaired almost 10,000 aircraft, including aircraft arriving at the Mersey docks from the USA. The first Sikorsky helicopters to be used by the Allies were also assembled and tested at Hooton Park towards the end of the war.

In June 1946, 610 Squadron reformed at Hooton, equipped with Spitfire Mark XIVs, then with Mark XXs and finally with Meteor Mark IV jet fighters. 663 Squadron also formed in 1949 with Tiger Moths and Auster 5 trainers, which were succeeded by De Havilland Chipmunks, and Auster 6s and

7s. Aircraft assembly and repair for both civil and military operators continued until the mid 1950s.

Hooton Park airfield finally closed in 1957, and in 1962, was purchased by Vauxhall Motors. The last aircraft to use the site, in 1988, were two Harriers which used part of the old runway prior to a display at an airshow nearby.

♦

9.

A FIGHTER IN MINIATURE

At Broughton on the Welsh side of the River Dee is the plant where the wings for Airbus airliners are made, including those for the A380, the largest airliner ever built. At Hooton, only a few miles away, nearly eighty years ago an enterprising former RAF Flight Lieutenant set up a company to build a diminutive, single-engine, single-seat aircraft of his own design.

Comper Aircraft Ltd was formed in 1929 by Nicholas ('Nick') Comper – one of four sons of the ecclesiastical architect Sir John Ninian Comper – at Hooton Park airfield, and he called his first aircraft design the 'Swift'. Designated the Comper CLA7, the prototype – registration G-AARX – made its first flight at Brooklands in Surrey on 17th May 1930.

Compared to the Airbus A380, with its wingspan of 261 ft 10 in (79.8m), length of 239 ft 6 in (73m), height of 79 ft 1 in (24,1 m) and four Rolls-Royce Trent 900 or General Electric/Pratt & Whitney GP-7200 turbofans engines, the Swift was absolutely minute. Most of the Swifts built were powered by the Pobjoy 'R' 75 hp seven cylinder radial engine. The aircraft had a wingspan of 24 feet (7.3 m) and was 18 feet (5.4 m) in length, 5 feet 2 inches (1.6 m) in height and had an all-up weight of just 985 lbs (447 kg). It cruised at 120 mph (190 kph) and had a maximum speed of 140 mph (225 kph). Its initial rate of climb was 1400 ft/min (70 m/sec) and it could reach an altitude of 22,000 ft (6,700 m). Using the standard fuel tank, its range was 380 miles (610 km). With its wings folded for storage or transport, the Swift would have fitted inside one of the A380's engine nacelles.

Seven more Swifts were completed during 1930, each powered by a Salmson AD 9 radial engine. However, a test flight with a prototype Pobjoy P radial engine led Comper to make it the standard power plant, and most of the earlier models were subsequently refitted with the Pobjoy engine. In total, forty-one of the standard Swifts were built. Choosing the Pobjoy engine was a sensible business decision, because during the 1920s and '30s Hooton Park was a busy industrial site that also housed the Pobjoy Aeroengine Company. Sales and demonstrations of the Compers were looked after by Brian Lewis & C D Barnard Ltd, another company based at the airfield.

Three Swifts were prepared specifically for racing; two with the 120 hp de Havilland Gipsy III engine and one with a 130 hp Gipsy Major. The Gipsy powered Swift was capable of more than 165 mph (265 kph) with a 140 mph (225 kph) cruising speed and a 1,400 ft/min (70m/sec) rate of climb. These were remarkable performance figures for such a low-powered machine, almost equal to those of contemporary fighter aircraft. In fact, the Swift was advertised as a 'fighter in miniature' and, costing £525, it was easily affordable. Advertisements said, "It doesn't tax your income. A Comper costs less to run than a baby car" (a small runabout like the Austin 7). It actually returned more than 25 miles to the gallon. Because of its ingenious folding wing design, it also had the advantage that it could be stored in a garage 9 feet (2.7 m) wide. The advertising also emphasised that, with the tailskid attached to a car towing-hook, it was possible to tow the aircraft on the road on its own wheels.

The wings hinged backwards from the rear spar of the wing for storage. When prepared for flight, the wing was locked in place by a steel pin that passed through the two parts of the front spar joint assembly. When hinged backwards, the wing was self supporting and kept in the locked position by clips. An ingenious but complicated mechanism enabled the wing to be folded without the aileron controls having to be disconnected.

In terms of 1930s aeronautical design, the Swift was 'state of the art'. Saving weight was critical, so very thin steel sheet was used, flanged to increase stiffness and, wherever possible, drilled with lightening holes. Nick Comper meticulously designed almost every metal component of the airframe with several lightening holes, some of them as small as a ¼" (0.63 cm) diameter.

Comper Aircraft Limited was a small company, and photographic records show that the woodwork and assembly was carried out by the company. What is not certain, however, is whether they also produced the many different metal components. It is possible, given the quantity involved, that their manufacture may well have been sub-contracted to engineering companies on the Hooton Park site. The cost of producing the metal parts may have been less considering that the necessary skills existed in the immediate vicinity.

The Comper Swift was different from other light aircraft of the 1930s in several respects. It is not obvious from the outside, but the fuselage is made in three sections. The front, ahead of the leading edge of the wing, provided a straightforward mounting for the engine. One reason for the relatively wide range of engines which were fitted was the ease with which the front section could be altered. Seven different engines were used in the forty-one Swifts built between 1930 and 1934, including the ABC Scorpion 40 hp fitted to the prototype G-AARX, Salmson AD9 54 hp, Pobjoy P 50 hp, Pobjoy R 75 hp, Pobjoy Niagara 90 hp and the two de Havilland engines.

The 'Swift' was in the headlines more than once in the early 1930s. It first grabbed the attention of the public when, in 1931, Charles Butler, described by the press as "one of the smallest pilots in the British Empire" and the "carpet-slippered airman", made an incredible, record-breaking flight to Australia. He left Lympne on the Kent coast on 31st October and reached Naples before refuelling. From there he flew in stages until he reached Darwin in the Northern Territories on 9th November after 105 hours in the air. Because his Swift carried extra fuel, Butler's baggage was limited to 1½ lbs (0.68 k) not including the famous carpet slippers that he wore for flying! It was testimony to the endurance of the aircraft and engine, and Butler himself, that he followed his flight with a tour of Australia that covered not far short of a further 2,300 miles (3,700 km) before, finally, the Swift was crated up and shipped back to England. The following year another pilot, Charles Taylor, crossed the Andes twice in a Pobjoy-powered Swift without oxygen, reaching an altitude of more than 15,000 feet (4,572 m).

Two of the de Havilland powered aircraft were unveiled only a couple of weeks before the King's Cup air race of 1932. The first was the Prince of Wales' aircraft, G-ABWW, painted in the Guards' colours of red and blue, with the 130 hp Gipsy Major engine. It joined the Prince's existing fleet of personal aircraft which included a DH 84 Dragon,

Above:
Charles Butler
reaches Sydney
in G-ABRE in 1931

Left:
Advertisement for the
Comper Swift

DH 83 Fox Moth and a DH 89 Dragon Rapide. The other Gipsy powered Swift was G-ABWH, with the 120 hp Gipsy III. Eight Swifts altogether were entered for the race at Brooklands on 7th July. The race was won by W L Hope in a Fox Moth, G-ABUT, and the Swift, G-ABWW, flown by Flt Lt Edward Fielden, the Prince of Wales' equerry, came second. The Prince's aircraft also competed in the 1933 and 1934 King's Cup races, and the Cleveland Race in Ohio, USA, in 1934.

One of the Gipsy powered Swifts ended up in Australia, and took part in the Ansett Brisbane to Adelaide Air Race of 1964. It was G-ABWH, with the 120 hp engine, which by then was owned by Edward Fielden himself, who had been knighted and had reached the rank of Air Vice-Marshal. It was said that the aircraft, which had then flown not much more than 230 hours since being built, "still flew like a dream".

One of the most famous Swifts, which carried the manufacturer's number S 32/9 (the ninth Swift to be built in 1932), was 'Scarlet Angel', with the Indian registration VT-ADO. The aircraft, fitted with a Pobjoy 75 hp 'R' engine, was ordered by Alban Ali, a tea planter in Assam. After the aircraft was shipped to India, Ali set out to fly from Calcutta to England, taking time out to compete in the Viceroy's Cup air race in Delhi, where he set the second fastest time for the 699 mile (1,125 km) course, at a speed of 124 mph (199.5 kph). Resuming the flight to England, Ali was forced to land in Egypt by engine failure. The aircraft was shipped to England where it was sold by its disappointed pilot and re-registered as G-ACTF. In 1950 it was flown into fifth place in the Daily Express air race, establishing an FAI class record speed of 141 mph (226.9 kph), a remarkable performance for an eighteen year old aircraft.

Along with three other Swifts in the United Kingdom, 'Scarlet Angel' is still in flying condition. It had been privately owned by Alan Chalkley, who had the aircraft completely refurbished before it was bought by the Shuttleworth Trust, based at Old Warden Aerodrome, near Biggleswade in Bedfordshire, in 1996, to add to its collection of pre-war light aircraft, and it is now a popular performer in flying displays at Old Warden.

In addition to the Swift, Comper built three other designs: the 'Mouse', a three-seat touring aircraft with an enclosed cabin which first flew on 10th September 1933. A low wing monoplane with retractable main landing gear and a tailskid, it was powered by a 130 hp DH Gipsy Major engine. Its wingspan was 37 ft 6 in (11.4 m), its length 25 ft 1 in (7.6 m). It had an all-up weight of 2,215 lb (1,004.7 k) and a cruising speed of 130 mph (209 kph). There are no known surviving examples.

Next came the 'Streak' which first flew on 12th April 1934. A single-seat sporting low wing monoplane, the pilot sat in an open cockpit. The Streak had an all wooden fuselage and a retractable undercarriage. Its 146 hp DH Gipsy Major high compression engine should have given it a performance to eclipse the Swift. However, it seems to have been a disappointment for one reason or another, and again no examples survive.

Finally, Comper came up with the 'Kite', which had its first flight in May 1934. For this two-seat touring version of the Streak with tandem open cockpits, surprisingly, the company reverted to a Pobjoy engine, the 90 hp 'Niagara', which gave it a maximum speed of 140 mph (227 kph).

Pobjoy Air Motors Limited, which had been founded by Douglas Pobjoy, moved from Hooton Park to Rochester in 1934 to be closer to Short Brothers, for whom they were contracted to produce the engine for the Short 'Scion'. Financial difficulties led Shorts to make a capital investment in Pobjoy, and the company was eventually absorbed into Shorts. In Pobjoy's relatively short independent life, its small and efficient radial engines powered nearly forty different types of light single- and twin-engine aircraft. Douglas Pobjoy himself successfully switched to designing tractors at the end of World War II, but tragically he was killed when a Douglas DC-6 and an Avro York collided on approach to Northolt airport in 1948.

At the end of 1934 the Heston Aircraft Company acquired Comper's assets and the Comper company left Hooton Park. Heston Aircraft was based at Heston Airport near Hounslow, from where the first commercial air services to Paris started. In 1938 Heston began building two examples of the Napier-Heston Racer, designed to prise the world air speed record from the Germans. War broke out before construction was finished, but the company was ordered to complete one of the pair of racers. Unfortunately, it crashed during its maiden flight and was destroyed. It was probably the last aircraft designed by the company. During World War II, when de Havilland exhausted its production capacity, it passed the design and development of the twin-engine "Sea Hornet" fighter to the Heston Aircraft Company. The company also undertook production of aero engines and other components for various aircraft manufacturers.

Sadly, Nick Comper was killed in 1939, but something of his heritage lives on, not just in the handful of original

Swifts still flying, but also in the form of a Comper Swift metalwork kit produced by Aviation Metalcraft Limited, which comprises some 480 individual parts and is currently the only kit available for building an airworthy vintage aircraft anywhere in the world. The kit has been produced from the original 1930s Comper Aircraft factory drawings, the majority of which still exist. There are some 250 drawings, representing 95% of the drawings made for the Swift. Fortunately, Aviation Metalwork has been able to make replacements for missing drawings by being given access to G-ACTF 'Scarlet Angel' the original Swift owned by the Shuttleworth Collection. Should anyone wish to recreate this nimble and characterful little aircraft, they will find it is quite possible to do so.

♦

10.
A MEDIAEVAL SAILORS' HOSPITAL

For nearly four hundred years St Andrew's Hospital stood, close to the marshy shoreline at Denhall between Burton and Ness. It had been established in the early 1230s to help the poor and the survivors of shipwrecks by Alexander Stavensby, the Bishop of Coventry and Lichfield, in whose diocese it was. The hospital stood by an inlet which served as a small fishing port, which was probably the reason for its dedication to St Andrew, the patron saint of fishermen.

Bishop Stavensby annexed the hospital to the nearby church of St Mary and St Helen, Burton. This meant that instead of paying a tithe to Lichfield Cathedral, as Burton had traditionally done, the parish would now pay that money to maintain the new hospital. The Dean and Chapter of Lichfield were given the tithes of Tarvin church, on the other side of Chester, in compensation, and they duly confirmed the annexation and the Bishop's appropriation of Burton church to his hospital in 1238. Pope Gregory IX gave his approval to the arrangement in 1241.

The hospital was referred to in the 13th Century as a secular priory, meaning that it was also a religious community of monks who had not been ordained priest. In the year 1251 the Pope confirmed the liberties and privileges of the prior and brethren. The Prior made a grant of land in Burton round about the same time, the wording of which implied that the community was mixed at that period, since the grant states that it is "by the wish and consent of the brethren and sisters there serving God". It is the only known reference to women living in the hospital.

On the appointment of William de Chaveley as Warden in 1320, Bishop Walter Langton confirmed the existing constitution of the hospital, which required the new Warden together with two resident priests to wear the customary 'decent dress' with a cross and to ensure that masses and other services were celebrated regularly. The Warden was to act as hospitaller in admitting poor men, travellers arriving from Ireland, and others. (A hospitaller was someone charged with aiding the sick, i e giving them hospice.) Even in the early days, however, it is unlikely that the Warden would have resided permanently at Denhall. In the 1260s the Prior of St Andrew's was appointed deputy to the Bishop's Warden and also acted as the Warden of the nuns of Chester.

From about 1300 the Wardenship of the hospital, which was valued at £10 a year, was usually vested not in an individual but in a group of secular clerks, several of whom were prebendaries either of Lichfield Cathedral or of St. John's, Chester.

Little is known of the history of the hospital in the later Middle Ages, apart from the names of the Masters. William de Newhagh was said to have improved the buildings and increased the income of the poor inmates. He had been Warden for twenty-five years before resigning the Mastership in 1400 on grounds of age and ill-health; he was granted an annual pension of 10 marks.

In January 1496 the hospital at Denhall was united by the Bishop of Lichfield with the newly rebuilt and re-founded Hospital of St John the Baptist in Lichfield, as it was regarded as too impoverished to continue independently. The last recorded Warden of St Andrew's was John Bothe,

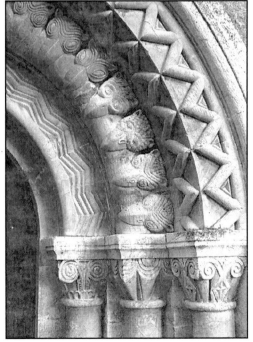

*Above: Hospital
of St. Cross
Winchester.
St. Andrew's
Hospital may have
looked something
like this*

Left:
Detail of a Norman
doorway

who was appointed in1449. In 1499, after the hospital had ceased its independent existence, extensive privileges, which may have dated from the foundation of St Andrew's, were claimed by the Master of St John's. These included free fishing in the Dee within the hospital bounds, the right of wreck (i e impounding anything of value that washed ashore from a shipwreck), and a warren of rabbits (kept for meat) on the hospital lands.

From early days, quays had been built by the hospital and seem to have been heavily used by people transporting goods to and from Chester. They would also have been used for offloading goods for Chester from seagoing vessels riding at anchor on the river. The privileges claimed in 1499 also included giving the Master the right to claim tolls on merchandise landed there. The Master had the right to carry corn and other necessities in the small boat belonging to the hospital free of toll. Sheriffs and other officials could not enter the lands or waters of the hospital to exercise their offices and the Master claimed to be under the special protection of the Earl of Chester.

R W Morant, author of "Monastic and Collegiate Cheshire", believes that the site of St Andrew's may have continued to be used as a hospital until its remaining inmates died, finally closing probably some time before 1547.

The site of the Denhall hospital, which formed the most valuable part of the estate of St. John's Hospital, was leased after the union to Sir Thomas Smith of Hough. The buildings seem to have been used as the parsonage house of Burton church. In the 17th Century the Masters of St. John's tended to treat the former hospital as their personal property and in 1675 Francis Ashenhurst settled the site of the Denhall hospital and the glebe and tithes of Burton on his future wife. The estate and the valuable privileges granted in 1499, remained in the hands of the Ashenhurst family and in 1738, with the permission of the bishop and the master of St. John's, part of the hospital buildings were demolished and a new parsonage house was built closer to the Burton church. In 1751 the remains of the hospital buildings, then in a ruinous state, were demolished, apart from one outlying building which had been converted into a barn. Some remains were still visible above ground in 1897 and stone from the buildings was incorporated in a wall which bordered the field, known as 'Chapel Field', where the hospital once stood.

Although only the earthworks remained, the site was designated a Scheduled Ancient Monument in 1975. In 1996 it was acquired by Ellesmere Port and Neston Borough Council, with the help of grants from Cheshire County Council and English Heritage.

A measured survey of the surviving earthworks, together with a geophysical survey of features below the surface, was carried out by Cheshire Archaeology in 1999. It revealed the outlines of the chapel and the infirmary, the drainage system and the outbuildings of the hospital. The archaeologists also found a previously unsuspected trackway, a perimeter wall around the hospital precinct, and a series of probable mediaeval quays at the mouth of the inlet from the River Dee.

The only other mediaeval hospitals known to have existed on Wirral were the house of lepers which gave its name to the hamlet of Spital, and another said to have stood on the boundary between the Wirral manors of Irby and

Thurstaston. In 1283 the brethren of the Bebington leper house were licensed to enclose and cultivate part of the forest of Wirral in order to support the community of that hospital. Today its precise location remains unknown. The hospital between Irby and Thursaston, mentioned at the beginning of the 14th Century probably only existed for a short time, like many leper hospitals, and left little in the way of remains.

◆

11.

HARD TIMES AND
THE BIRTH OF A LEGEND

In the early 19th Century one commentator, who had visited the Denhall coal mine near Ness, Wirral, said that it was the most miserable and desolate place he had ever seen. Not only men, but whole families, including small children, went underground for only a few pence a day. Not surprisingly, they also lived in squalid cottages which were alive with vermin and insects. Of all the people who worked in the colliery at Denhall, Wirral's first coal mine, the man who comes closest to fame is one Henry Lyon, but we will leave his story until later.

Some small scale extraction of coal in Wirral was recorded from as early as the 17th Century, but commercial mining did not begin until the 1700s. Ness was nothing more than a small farming hamlet until the Stanleys of Hooton opened the Denna (Denhall) Colliery in 1760, to extract coal from a seam which ran out under the Dee towards Flintshire. (It was the same seam that was mined from the colliery at Point of Air on the Welsh side of the Dee.) The Denhall shaft was located a few metres from Denhall Quay, one of a succession of quays built as the Dee silted up, and coal was shipped out from the quay to Chester and Liverpool. About two hundred yards (180 m) north of the pit was the miners' pub, the 'Harp Inn', which still offers a refreshing pint and a fine view over the Dee (and never a coal blackened face to be seen).

Working conditions even towards the end of the pit's life

were bad, but in the early years they were truly appalling, scarcely any better than slave labour. Boys began work there as early as seven years of age and everything was done using hands or feet. The Stanley family, the owners of the mine, living in elegant splendour at Hooton Hall, six miles (9.6 km) away, probably knew little and cared less about the lives of the miners scraping out a miserable living on the bleak shore of the River Dee.

The coal seam was thin and, in his "History of the Hundred of Wirral", William Mortimer describes how the poor quality coal was hauled to the bottom of the shaft in small boats along two underground canals. Each boat carried four hundredweight (0.2 tonne) of coal in baskets. Four or five of the boats would be roped together and then propelled along by a man lying on his back on the coal in the first boat. He would push with his feet against the tunnel roof, a method similar to that used to propel narrowboats through tunnels on the canals known as 'legging'. Denhall Colliery was closed round about 1855 when it became impossible to extract any more coal using such primitive and dangerous methods.

Perhaps at this point we should return to Henry Lyon. In 1764 he had married 21 year old Mary Kidd who came from Harwarden, and they had moved into Smith's Cottage (which still exists), near the road to Denhall, in Neston Road, Ness. Henry worked at Denhall Colliery although he also worked as the village blacksmith. The small house was one of a number of similar cottages that belonged to the Stanleys.

It was a hard life and Henry no doubt suffered from ill health like most of the miners, although at least some of his working time was spent above ground. Even men of twenty were bent by the backbreaking work within a few years of starting work; they had to crouch in muddy, icy water and hack at the sides of the flooded tunnels. Others died, poisoned by pockets of methane or killed by rock falls underground. Henry and Mary's daughter, Amy, was born on Friday, 26th April 1765. Her prospects were not good; her life promised to be poor and short. Two months after she was baptised, her father died suddenly. He was buried in June 1765 in the churchyard of St Mary and St Helen, the parish church of Neston.

No cause of death is recorded for Henry Lyon, and his grave is unmarked. Of course, the life expectancy of men who worked as miners was short, although their deaths from respiratory diseases could be agonising and long drawn out. But there is no record of an accident at Denhall, or of an epidemic of any kind, in the spring or summer of 1765. Mary did not receive a pension or compensation from the mine, which might have been the case if Henry had died at work there. Their baby daughter, as Kate Williams puts it in a recently published book, seemed "destined for a cruel and meagre life: backbreaking labour by the age of ten, a hard marriage, and an early death".

With nothing to keep her in Ness, Mary took her daughter back to her family in Harwarden, where the air was clean and the living conditions not so desperately poor. In time Amy, who preferred to be known as Emma, rose far above her humble beginnings. She married Sir William Hamilton, the British envoy to Naples from 1764 to 1800, and achieved lasting notoriety as the mistress of Admiral Horatio Nelson.

The end of the last shift at Denhall Colliery, 1928

Smith's Cottages, Ness village

Mining began again, not far away from Denhall, at a new location in Little Neston in the middle of the 19th century. There is evidence that when William Lever built his soap works at Port Sunlight, in 1888, at least some of the coal for the works was brought by rail from Little Neston. The coal owners were two brothers by the name of Platt, and the manager of the colliery was J S Taylor. Despite the fact that there were plenty of men who had worked at Denhall, they preferred to bring in skilled miners from North Wales, Lancashire and even Yorkshire rather than to recruit locally. This influx from other mining areas probably accounts for the fact that Neston developed a dialect noticeably different from the rest of Wirral.

Many mines up and down the country were forced to close in the slump of the 1920s and '30s. In an attempt to preserve mining on Wirral, attention turned to the defunct Denhall Colliery. In the hope that further reserves of coal could be found, two crews were lowered down the derelict shaft by a steam winch mounted on the back of a Sentinel steam wagon. They discovered that the canals, with arches cut through the coal, and some of the coal baskets and boats were still intact. However, this exhausting and hazardous system was replaced by ponies pulling tubs along on rails. Coal of poor quality was extracted for a short while before both the Little Neston and Denhall mines were finally abandoned in 1928. The shafts were sealed off, equipment was removed and the ponies, as well as the shire horses which had delivered household coal in the area were sold.

Today, the visible remains of Wirral's coal industry are the gorse- and grass-covered spoil heaps of the old colliery, one street of miners' terraced houses (New Street) and the

Harp Inn which last served a working miner eighty or more years ago. The inn has a number of framed photographs of the mine and those who worked there.

♦

12.

STRAINING TOWARDS
THE HEAVENS

Driving from the "Devon Doorway" along Telegraph Road into the prosperous but culturally conservative community of Heswall, visitors are startled to see on the left hand side an unconventional and uncompromisingly modern building rooted in an outcrop of red sandstone. With its tall, narrow upper windows on two façades and a soaring pointed roof, the building seems to be straining towards the heavens. And what could be more appropriate? For this is the Meeting House of Quakers in Heswall. Arguably, it is the most striking 20th Century building on Wirral.

The Quakers or, to give them their formal title, 'The Religious Society of Friends', trace their beginnings to the inspiration of George Fox, who was born in 1624 in a small village in Leicestershire called Fenny Drayton. The 17th Century was a period of political and religious upheaval. In 1642 civil war engulfed the country until, in 1649, Parliament executed the King (Charles I) who was succeeded by the Commonwealth under the Lord Protector, Oliver Cromwell.

During the Civil War years, the King's authority over the church was weakened, and ordinary people had unusual freedom to explore alternative religious ideas and practices. George Fox was disillusioned by the hypocrisy of ministers of the Established Church, whom he referred to as "so-called professors of the Christian faith". He left home and in his travels came across small groups of freethinkers some of whom called themselves 'Seekers'.

It was from these independent-minded groups, which coalesced around George Fox, that Quakerism grew.

A Meeting House had existed in Chester since the 17th Century, but it was not until 1854 that one was built on Wirral, in Withens Lane, Wallasey (now demolished). A second, still in use, was built not long afterwards in Slatey Road, Birkenhead. In 1937 a small group of Quakers began meeting in Heswall. Their early meetings were held in the vestry of Heswall Parish Hall. From 1939 the difficulties and dangers of travelling to Birkenhead in wartime conditions provided an added incentive for them to meet for worship near where they lived.

The little group met in a variety of premises in Heswall, until in 1952 they settled in the grand-sounding 'Milner Rooms', (actually a prefabricated hut in a builder's yard in Milner Road), where they remained for over ten years. In 1956, however, the Heswall Quakers began to look for a suitable site where they could build their own Meeting House.

Finding a suitable site proved to be a long and often frustrating process. Negotiations for one plot were delayed for nine months because the owner, in Canada, could not make up his mind to sell, in case a Meeting House would lower the tone of the neighbourhood!

Eventually, at the end of January 1958, an offer of £800 was made for a plot of land, which included an outcrop of sandstone, at the corner of North Drive and Telegraph Road. This land was also owned by an absentee owner and negotiations dragged on for nearly eight months until agreement was reached to buy the site for £905.

Left:
Quaker Meeting
House Heswall

Below:
Telegraph Road
and North Drive
1961

The choice of architect fell on Dewi Prys Thomas (1916-1985), a young architect on the staff of the Department of Architecture at Liverpool University, who was also in architectural practice in Liverpool with Gerald Beech.

Prys Thomas was a passionate and poetic Welsh Nonconformist, who could recite pages of the Bible from memory, but he had not had any previous connection with Quakers. He was born into a Welsh family who had moved to Liverpool and had been educated at the Liverpool Institute and Liverpool University. After graduating, he taught in Cardiff but was invited to return to Liverpool as a lecturer by the Professor of Architecture, Lionel Budden. His most noted work is the Gwynedd County Offices in Caernarfon.

Before engaging Prys Thomas, members of the Meeting went to see a Roman Catholic Church on Anglesey, and a house in Woolton, Liverpool, which he had designed as the 'Woman's Journal House of the Year'. They liked what they saw and asked him to design their new Meeting House. They felt that he had quickly grasped what Quakerism was about: when he produced a design that envisaged the Meeting House "built on a rock; stretching upwards to heaven".

Using the small site to maximum effect, Prys Thomas' design would lead worshippers on their arrival in a gradual approach to their meeting room, up the rocky site, round a projecting glass-clad drum and up a gently rising staircase to the 'upper room' of the Meeting House. In the meeting room itself, long slender windows, with views mainly of the sky, would lead the thoughts of worshippers upwards to the heavens. Apart from this strong Christian symbolism, having the silent Meeting for Worship in an 'upper room' was also, in practical terms, intended to lift it above the noise of passing traffic.

Planning permission for the Meeting House was granted by a "rather astonished" local council. By January 1959, an appeal for funds had been circulated within the Society of Friends. The appeal leaflet featured Prys Thomas' own sketch of the striking modern design which – plainness and simplicity being greatly valued by Quakers – came to be known humorously in Quaker circles as 'the Quaker cathedral'. "Quaker Faith and Practice", a book that contains both inspiration and practical advice, says:

"In the provision of Meeting Houses, [Quakers] should, wherever possible, choose sites which allow for the greatest possible use to the whole community... In considering the building of Meeting Houses [we] should have regard to the suitability of the building as a place of worship, simplicity of design and soundness of construction and to the avoidance of extravagance."

The main contractor for the Meeting House, which cost £12,800, was Mohin (Bebington) Ltd. It is on record that Mr Mohin was intrigued at the way the Quakers allowed both himself and the architect to get on with the work without interference; this reflected the enormous confidence that they had in them both.

The Meeting House opened on 19th April 1963. The "Birkenhead Advertiser" described it as "one of the most architecturally unusual buildings to be built in Heswall", which was more subtle that the name given to it by some local residents who referred to it as "the mortuary"! Despite this, the Meeting House was listed in Nikolaus Pevsner's definitive book "The Buildings of Cheshire" as one of only two buildings of interest in Heswall.

In his book, "Heswall Friends", John Noble makes it clear that the Meeting House has amply fulfilled the requirement that it should serve not just Quakers but the whole community:

"...The Meeting House has been 'home' for bee-keepers, townswomen, keep fit and slimming classes, guitar and piano tutors, University extension classes and many more local organisations."

But of course, for Heswall Quakers themselves, the life of the Meeting House revolves around the Meeting for Worship at 10.30 every Sunday morning, to which they warmly welcome people of all faiths and denominations or none.

♦

13.

FLAT WATER, STRONG WINDS

The Marine Lake is a distinctive feature of West Kirby, unthinkingly accepted by most residents of Wirral as, part of the landscape. Of course, they know that it is not a natural but a man-made salt water lake, but how many of them could put a date on its construction or, for that matter, say when the West Kirby Sailing Club, which is based there, was founded?

To put the origins of the lake in context; it was not until the last quarter of the 19th Century that West Kirby, and its near neighbour Hoylake, were anything more than fishing villages. In 1871 the two places together had no more than 2,118 residents, most of them in Hoylake. On the First Edition of the Ordnance Survey (OS) map, West Kirby consisted or only four or five buildings at the junction of Grange Road and Dee Lane. Thirty years later, however, the combined population of West Kirby and Hoylake had reached 10,991. By the time the Second Edition of the OS was published in 1897, the layout of the village south of Grange Road was more or less as it appears today, and by 1900 the shops on the north side of the road had been built.

The cause of this explosive growth was the arrival of the railway. The first railway along the northern end of the Wirral peninsula had been the Hoylake Railway, opened in 1866, but it did not reach as far as West Kirby. Not surprisingly, it was not a success since the area it served was, at that time, mostly sparsely populated marshland and sand dunes. Within four years the company was in the hands of bailiffs. However, in 1872 the line was bought by the Hoylake and Birkenhead Railway Company, newly formed for the purpose, which extended it to West Kirby in 1878.

Developers finally recognised the potential of West Kirby's location, and the place grew out of all recognition. The railway offered the possibility of working in Birkenhead or Liverpool and escaping to the clean air and peaceful surroundings of Wirral in the evenings and at weekends – commuting was born! In addition, and with the railway company's encouragement, those residents of Liverpool who could not afford to live on Wirral could at least take day trips or holidays "over the water", and lodging houses and hotels sprang up to cater for them.

One of the biggest of these was the large and imposing Hydropathic Hotel, built round about 1890 and further extended in 1896. Popularly known as 'the Hydro', the hotel advertised baths including "Turkish, Russian, Electric, Nauheim, Seaweed, Salt Water, Plunge, etc"; one wonders about the health-giving properties, not to say the method of operation of the Electric Bath!

By June 1895 there was talk of building a marine lake, like those that had already been built at Southport and Rhyl. In September the same year the West Kirby Improvement Association had been set up, and a year later a Bill was introduced in Parliament to authorise the building of a continuous promenade from Hoylake to West Kirby, deepening the Hoyle Lake and building a marine lake at West Kirby. The Bill became law in March 1897 and construction began shortly afterwards.

The original plan was for a marine lake three-quarters of a mile (1.2 km) long and 150 yards (137 m) wide. Design and construction of both the lake and the promenade was entrusted to the Borough Engineer, Thomas Foster. His original estimate for the cost of the lake's construction had been £2,500. Because of changes demanded by the Council it actually cost £3,500, for which Foster was heavily criticised in some quarters, although even its final cost was about a tenth of what the lake at Southport had cost. It was fortunate, also, that although both Hoylake and West Kirby got their promenades the intervening section was never built.

The Marine Lake was built on the shore in front of the Hydropathic Hotel. The hotel itself had closed in 1895 but it reopened a year later when its proprietors realised that the Marine Lake would attract many more visitors to the town. The lake opened on 21st October 1899 and, as built, it included an open-air swimming pool which has long since gone. It has been popular with sailing enthusiasts ever since, because of its unique combination of flat water and strong prevailing winds. The lake covers an area of 52 acres (21 hectares) and is no more than five feet (1.5 m) deep, which also makes it ideal for those who are learning to sail.

Not long after the lake was opened, a small group of gentlemen decided to form a sailing club. The West Kirby Sailing Club (WKSC) was formed in 1901. In its early days the club used a room in the Hydropathic Hotel for its meetings, but later it moved into its own clubhouse and raced on the marine lake in 12ft (3.6 m) dinghies.

A new purpose-built clubhouse was built in 1953 which, with some alterations, is still in use today. Racing took

The sea wall, West Kirby Marine Lake

Probable site of the former Hydropathic Hotel

place both on the Marine Lake and on the River Dee until, in 1985, the retaining wall of the lake was breached. The WKSC came up with a plan to effect temporary repairs, and it was WKSC members who carried out the work of repairing the hole in the wall so that racing could continue. Unfortunately the repairs did not last long and the wall gave way again. In 1986, with the Marine Lake out of commission, racing could only take place on the River Dee.

Plans were drawn up for a new Marine Lake. The WKSC lobbied hard, not only to have the lake reinstated, but to have it extended and its facilities improved. In 1987 the new lake was opened, with a greatly extended boat yard, pontoons and new slipways.

In addition to the WKSC, there is a chandlery and Sailing School which provides Royal Yachting Association courses in sailing, windsurfing and canoeing. The lake is home to a number of sailing clubs, schools and events including the Wilson Trophy, the premier UK team sailing competition, which has been held at West Kirby for the last fifty years. It is one of the biggest team sailing events in the world and extremely prestigious. Teams from all over the world compete in the event, which frequently attracts the World Team Racing champions. The lake is also used by windsurfers and canoeists from all over the North West and beyond.

As part of a regeneration plan for West Kirby, Wirral Borough Council has concluded that the facilities are no longer satisfactory, particularly for hosting regional, national and international events. According to a report to the Council's Economic Regeneration and Planning Strategy Committee in November 2004:

"The current Sailing School building is in a poor state of repair, does not include the modern facilities necessary to satisfactorily deliver national and international events and certainly does not make the most of the stunning coastline and views across the Dee Estuary... there is no youth hostel style accommodation and insufficient budget accommodation to house watersports visitors to the Marine Lake... The Lake is also a highly popular destination for promenading, birdwatching, and summer relaxation and there are currently very few facilities available to these visitors".

The Borough Council therefore proposes to redevelop the Sailing School. This project has been called 'The Sail', to reflect the prestige of the sailing and wind surfing events on the Marine Lake. The development will incorporate innovative and striking architecture appropriate to a sensitive location, and a focal point for the town of West Kirby and the Dee Estuary.

However, the 2004 report also noted that, "Further consultation, feasibility and design work will be necessary to realise the proposed key projects. Equally other projects may come forward that fit the vision and strategy." In other words, it would be as well not to hold your breath. Unless, that is, the West Kirby Sailing Club is as effective in lobbying today as it was in 1985, when it succeeded in persuading the Borough Council not only to repair but to extend and improve the Marine Lake in just two years!

◆

14.

WATERWAYS
THAT ARE AND AREN'T

The Wirral peninsula, between the River Mersey and the River Dee, is roughly 60.35 square miles (156.3 sq km) in area. Two hundred million years ago, when the whole of the British Isles was much closer to the Equator than it is today, Wirral had not yet formed. Between the mountains of Snowdonia and the Pennine hills was a wide, sandy delta. Over millions of the ensuing years, in the process called geomorphology, geological processes transformed the expanse of sand into rock, known as Triassic Sandstone. Subsequent movements of the earth's crust thrust up some of the rock to form two parallel ridges, varying only slightly in height from 220 to 300 feet (67 to 91 m).

The more easterly ridge extends from Bidston Hill to Storeton Ridge, while the westerly ridge runs from West Kirby in the north-west to Burton in the south west of Wirral, with just one dip at Dawpool, between Caldy and Thurstaston. Centuries ago the sea flowed through this valley, which extended as far as Moreton and Bidston, making an island (Wallasey, i e 'island of the strangers') of the north western corner of Wirral.

For such a small area, some twelve miles (19.3 km) long by seven miles (11.2 km) wide, Wirral has had more than its fair share of projected canals. At least six canals have been planned, of which only two (the Ellesmere Canal from Chester to Ellesmere Port and the Manchester Ship Canal) were actually built. The earliest of all these schemes was the Wirral section of the Ellesmere Canal surveyed by Telford on which work began in 1794. Next came a survey for a ship canal in 1823-1824 by a Scottish engineer called Robert Stevenson. This was intended to be capable of taking 400 ton (362.8 tonne) vessels, from Dawpool, through the gap in the westerly sandstone ridge, heading south and then east past Frodsham, Lymm and Didsbury to approach Manchester from the south. It was promoted by a group of Chester merchants, whose concern was to bolster the city's position as a port against that of Liverpool. By starting from the Dee estuary the canal would bypass Liverpool entirely and enable seagoing ships to avoid the more difficult sections of the upper Mersey & Irwell Navigation to Manchester. The plan came to nothing, however, when the enabling Bill was rejected by Parliament. The men of Chester and Wirral were nothing if not persistent, and variations of the plan for a ship canal were put forward in 1825, 1826, 1828 and 1837 but the canal never received the assent of Parliament and was never built.

In fact, in 1825 two separate canals were projected. The first proposal was for a relatively modest canal, surveyed by Telford and Stevenson, again to be entered from the Dee at Dawpool and connecting with the Mersey at Wallasey Pool. Once again, this was squashed by the opposition of Liverpool Corporation combined with the advancing silting-up of the Dee estuary.

The second proposal that year was another attempt to build a ship canal 51 miles (82 km) in length, to carry vessels up to 250 tons (226.7 tonnes) from the River Dee to Manchester. This time it was the work of William Chapman (most of whose other work was in Ireland and

*Above: The Chester
Canal at Stoak*

*Left:
Lighthouse and
entrance lock,
Ellesmere Port*

Yorkshire) assisted by Richard Buck and Ralph Burton. It was Chapman's opinion that such a canal would be big enough to handle the majority of vessels at that time using the port of Liverpool (he estimated that about 2,120 vessels out of 3,240 were of less than 100 tons). Cargo from vessels bigger than 250 tons would be transhipped at the docks that he proposed to build at Dawpool on the Dee. He estimated the cost of the canal to be £1,569,000.

It seems likely, from the contours of the land, that Chapman intended to deepen the existing channel that drains Dawpool Bank at low tide and then to begin cutting the canal by following the line of the stream that flows from a small wood, known as The Dungeon, down to the Dee. After that, the line would probably have followed that of the Fender brook, using it as a feeder, and then joined the route later taken by the M53 Motorway. Since civil engineers, whether they are building canals, railways or roads, have usually come to very similar conclusions as to the most desirable route, it may not be too fanciful to suggest that Chapman's Manchester & Dee Canal would have anticipated much of the route of the M53 and then of the M56 to south Manchester.

A Bill was duly introduced in Parliament, but it was opposed and thrown out on standing orders. As it was, the canal would have been unable, without substantial and expensive improvements to keep pace with the growth in the average size of ships, and it would have been more or less useless by within fifty years.

In 1826 Mr Dumbell of Mersey Mills, Warrington, while not opposing Chapman's scheme to provide Manchester with a connection with the sea, wrote a pamphlet which proposed that the Mersey also needed improvement to Warrington by the building of a barrage and locks at Runcorn Gap. Dumbell's suggestion was taken further in 1837, when a group of local businessmen commissioned a survey by John Rennie, who proposed a ship canal 16 ft (4.8 m) deep between Liverpool and Warrington that could if necessary be extended to Manchester without too much difficulty. Yet again, however, the plan came to nothing.

In 1828 Thomas Telford, who had already surveyed the Ellesmere Canal, returned to Wirral and, together with Alexander Nimmo and Robert Stevenson, reported on a scheme for a seven mile (11.2 km) ship canal running from a point opposite Hilbre Island off West Kirby parallel to the north coast of Wirral to Wallasey. The two principal aims of the scheme were to enable ships to avoid the difficult Mersey entrance channels, and to establish new docks at either end of the canal, at Hilbre on the River Dee and Wallasey on the River Mersey. In their report they stressed that, in their opinion, the dominant port of the North West should continue to be either on the Dee or the Mersey, adding that Liverpool was "not only the great mart of the North West of Britain and all of Ireland, but nearly of the whole western world".

Their wide-ranging plans mentioned that the main anchorage points in the Mersey at that time: were "off the Magazines" (at New Brighton) for outward bound vessels, and "up the river in Sloynes Roads (off New Ferry) or Brumbro (Bromborough) Pool which is almost confined to vessels under quarantine". They also discussed the possibility of making Wallasey Pool an anchorage site for larger vessels.

These plans were nothing if not ambitious in their scope. They included the building of a 'floating harbour' seven miles (11.2 km) long with warehouses. Including sea locks and the docks, the ship canal would have cost almost £1½ million, the equivalent today of more than £76 million. A less ambitious plan with fewer works was also outlined at an estimated cost of £750,000 or the equivalent of £38 million today. Sadly, even the engineers' more limited plans far outran the willingness of those who had commissioned them to risk their capital, and the plan was stillborn.

After that efforts were concentrated on the enlargement and straightening of the Mersey & Irwell Navigation in the 1840s until a Manchester businessman called Daniel Adamson proposed the hugely ambitious Manchester Ship Canal (MSC) in 1882. Work began on the MSC five years later, engineered by Edward Leader Williams. Unlike the earlier ship canal proposals, the MSC, was constructed from Eastham along the Mersey shoreline of Wirral and, further upriver, it obliterated and effectively canalized parts of both the Mersey and the Irwell.

Even that gigantic triumph of late 19th Century engineering has succumbed to the effect of the continued growth in the average size of seagoing vessels. The red-hulled 'Manchester Liners', so familiar in the 1960s and '70s, have long since made their last voyages, and the Salford Docks have shed their original purpose in favour of cultural, commercial and residential complexes. The placid water is little more than an attractive 'water feature'.

Lower down the canal, particularly at Runcorn, Ellesmere Port and Eastham but also at a number of smaller wharves, (the MSC has been described as being more of a linear dock than a canal), cargoes of cars, oil, chemicals, bulk cement and grain are still handled. For the owner, Peel Holdings (successor to the Manchester Ship Canal Company) the income generated by the Ship Canal is now a relatively minor part of its diversified business. Ultimately, the chief guarantee of the MSC's survival into the 21st Century is the fact that is an integral part of the land drainage for the Mersey Basin.

◆

15.

NOT TOO BAD A PLACE TO BE

Clatterbridge Hospital is probably best known today for its Centre for Oncology which provides radiotherapy and chemotherapy for people with cancer from Merseyside, Cheshire and the Isle of Man, but from 1836 until 1930 it was the site of the Workhouse of the Wirral Poor Law Union.

The Poor Law Unions were set up under an Act of Parliament which received Royal Assent on 14th August 1834. A Poor Law Commission was responsible for administering the new regime which replaced a hotch-potch of provision for poor relief that had grown up over centuries.

The Wirral Poor Law Union came into being on 23rd April 1836. It was overseen by an elected board of fifty-seven Guardians representing its 56 constituent parishes. Rev Mark Coxon was the first Chairman and William and Jane Redding were appointed as the first Master and Matron of the Workhouse.

The Poor Law Commissioners authorised the expenditure of £2,500 on the building of a new workhouse at Clatterbridge, designed by William Cole, to accommodate 130 inmates. It was financed by a loan from Rev Robert Mosley Feilden, the Rector of St Andrew's, Bebington. The building was economically furnished: the furniture cost £64.8s.0d in total. The Board Room contained only a deal table and twelve rush-bottomed chairs. A number of double-beds were purchased, each of which was to be occupied by three children.

The workhouse was like a small self-contained village. Apart from the dining-hall and dormitories, it had its own bakery, laundry, tailor's and shoe-maker's workshops, vegetable gardens, an orchard and even a piggery. There were also school-rooms, nurseries, wards for the sick, a chapel, and a mortuary.

The original water supply seems to have come from the Clatter Brook, but in 1839 an order was issued to sink a well. The workman who did the job was given a week to do it and was paid £2 5s 6d. At first no baths were provided – such luxuries were unknown to the working class. However, following the recommendation of the Medical Officer in 1840, the Guardians instructed the Master and Matron to "take the children [but not the adults!] to bathe at Bromberrow (Bromborough)."

By the time of the 1881 Census the Master of the Workhouse was Theophilus Tuck, aged 38, and his wife Olivia, aged 29, was the Matron. On the day of the Census there were 108 residents, the oldest being Samuel Nolan, aged 84, a farm labourer from Neston, and the youngest John Taigh who was just 9 months old. Of those whose occupation was recorded, 28 were schoolchildren; 22 were labourers (of whom 7 were farm labourers). There were 7 servants of one kind or another, 2 painters, 1 sailor from Ireland, 1 fisherman, 1 stone quarryman (who no doubt had worked at Storeton), 1 man who had been a coal miner at Ness, 1 plasterer, 1 baker's apprentice, 1 gardener, 1 coach trimmer, 1 tinker, 1 shoemaker, 1 barman, 1 brickmaker, 1 fisherman from the Isle of Man and a weaver from Stockport. There were just seven members of staff, including the Master and Matron, a Schoolmistress and her assistant, a Nurse and a married couple who were Porter and Portress.

Workhousestone yard

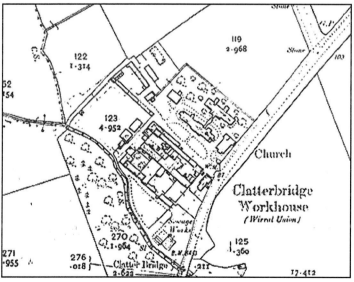

Map of Clatterbridge Workhouse 1908

People ended up in the workhouse for various reasons. Usually, it was because they were too poor, old or ill to support themselves. This might be the result of a lack of work during periods of high unemployment, or of having no family willing or able to provide for them when they became old or sick. Unmarried pregnant women were often disowned by their families and the workhouse was the only place to which they could go until the child was born. Before the establishment of mental asylums in the mid 19th Century those who were mentally ill or mentally handicapped were often consigned to the workhouse. The Workhouse, though, was not a prison, and people entered it voluntarily if reluctantly. However, it did have one thing in common with a prison: until 1918 being in receipt of poor relief meant that a person lost the right to vote.

Applicants for admission were interviewed by the Union's visiting Relieving Officer to establish their circumstances. However, the workhouse Master could admit anyone in urgent need. Admission to the workhouse proper was authorised by the Board of Guardians at their weekly meetings, where an applicant might be summoned to justify their application. Before being formally admitted to the main workhouse, new arrivals were allocated to the receiving ward, where the Medical Officer examined them. Those who were ill were placed in the sick ward. Once they entered the workhouse, paupers were stripped, bathed and issued with a workhouse uniform. Their own clothes were washed and disinfected and put into store, along with any other possessions they had, and only returned when they left the workhouse. By 1900, male inmates were provided with a jacket, trousers and a waistcoat. In later years, the uniform for able-bodied women was a shapeless, waistless, blue-and-white-striped frock reaching to the ankles, with a smock worn over it.

Inmates were divided into seven classes: Aged or Infirm men; Able-bodied Men, and Youths above 13; Youths and Boys above seven years old and under 13; Aged or Infirm women; Able-bodied Women and Girls above 16; Girls above seven years old and under 16; Children under 7 seven years of age. Each class had its own section of the workhouse. Husbands, wives and children were separated when they entered the workhouse and could be punished if they even tried to speak to one another. Children under seven could be placed (if the Guardians thought fit) in the female wards. From 1842, their mothers could have access to them "at all reasonable times". Parents could also have an "interview" with their children "at some time in each day". From 1847 married couples over the age of sixty could ask to share a separate bedroom.

The inmates' day began at 6.00 am from the end of March to the end of September, and at 7.00 am from then until the following March. Half an hour was allowed for breakfast then they would work until midday, have an hour for lunch and work until 6.00 pm, summer and winter. At 6.00 they had an hour for supper followed by an hour's free time before going to bed.

There was a variety of work to be done, much of it to do with running the workhouse. The women did domestic work such as cleaning or helping in the kitchen or laundry; others worked in the vegetable gardens. As Clatterbridge was a rural area able-bodied male inmates were sometimes used as labourers on neighbouring farms. Other work included breaking stone for road-mending; grinding corn, chopping firewood and oakum picking (teasing out the fibres from old hemp ropes) the product of which was sold to ship-builders. Mixed with tar it was used to seal the gaps between the planking of ships.

There can be few, if any, people still living who spent time in Clatterbridge Workhouse, but stories have been passed down in families. One woman says, "My Great Grandmother was in the Clatterbridge Workhouse with her parents in 1891. She left and married but her parents both died there in 1891 and 1906. My mother was in Clatterbridge when it was a hospital in the late 1960s and died there in 1970. My sister gave birth to her first child there, also in 1970. I remember visiting the hospital and the wards were old by then.

"From what I've heard it wasn't too bad a place to be. There was no central control hub and it appears that families were kept together as much as possible. When my Great-great grandparents died they were buried in their own home church in Neston... My Great-great Grandmother had been ill for some time and was cared for in the Workhouse infirmary. My Great Grandmother was given a good education; she could read, write, do arithmetic and had been taught to sew.

"A lot of misconceptions exist about the Workhouses and, while it was true not all of them were great places to be, many of them provided good sustenance and shelter for needy people."

After the workhouse system ended in 1930, the Wirral Workhouse was renamed Clatterbridge (County) General Hospital, and when the National Health Service was inaugurated on 5th July 1948 it became Clatterbridge Hospital. The last of the original workhouse buildings were finally demolished in 1997.

◆

16.

A LOST
ARCHITECTURAL TREASURE

Bebington has a remarkable forgotten link with some of the most iconic buildings in the country – including Buckingham Palace. Like them, the now demolished "Brackenwood", the grounds of which form the first nine holes of Brackenwood golf course, was designed by Sir Aston Webb who was born in 1849, and was one of the most successful and prolific architects in Edwardian Britain.

The site of "Brackenwood", was bought by John Evans of Evans Medical Limited. His grandfather, also named John, and great uncle Edward Evans had established themselves as chemists at 12 Foregate Street, Worcester, in the early 1800s. John Evans (the grandfather) had greater ambitions however, and left Worcester for London to become a wholesale chemist. Eventually he became the founder of Evans Medical Limited, a Liverpool based manufacturer and supplier of drugs and medical equipment. Webb built a factory in Wood Street in Liverpool for the Evans Medical company, (which is the only remaining example of his work on Merseyside, although now converted into apartments by Urban Splash).

Evans Medical is now part of the world-wide drug manufacturing conglomerate Medeva PLC, and is the only manufacturer of human vaccines in the U.K., including Fluvirin, a vaccine against influenza, as well as a range of childhood and travel vaccines. Evans Medical has also been a major supplier of childhood vaccines to international health organisations on whose behalf it exports to over a hundred countries. Employing over 600 people, the company has facilities in Speke, Liverpool, and three other sites in England. The company also manufactures and markets a range of branded pharmaceutical products.

John Evans (the grandson) had "Brackenwood" designed and built in 1885 by Aston Webb, who was his brother-in-law. Webb, at that time aged 36, received his architectural training when he was articled in the firm of Edward Banks and Charles Barry junior (son of Sir Charles Barry) from 1866 to 1871. The son of the water-colourist, Edward Webb, Aston was born in London. After qualifying, he spent a year travelling in Europe and Asia and set up his own architectural practice when he returned to London in 1874. One of his earliest works was a group of almshouses in the Arts & Crafts style built for the Six Masters of The Royal Grammar School, Worcester, in 1877. Later he and Ingress Bell (1836–1914) formed a partnership and carried out many important commissions. Their first major commission was the winning design for the brightly coloured Victoria Law Courts in Birmingham (1886), the first of numerous public buildings the pair designed over the next twenty-three years. The firm's office was at 15 Queen Anne Gate in Westminster.

Webb was the architect of many important London buildings around the turn of the 20th Century. His numerous public commissions included the Cromwell Road frontage of the Victoria & Albert Museum (1891). He received many honours including the Grand Cross of the Victorian Order (GCVO), and was President both of the Royal Institute of British Architects (RIBA) from 1902 to 1904, and of the Royal Academy from 1919 to 1924. He designed the eastern facade of Buckingham Palace (1913) and Admiralty Arch (1908-1909), as well as laying out The Mall as a formal processional way, terminating at the Victoria Monument. The Royal United Services Institute, in Whitehall (1893-1895) and the Metropolitan Life Assurance building in Moorgate are also his.

Outside London, he designed the Royal Naval College at Dartmouth, Devon (1899-1904), where Royal Navy officers are still trained, and the University of Birmingham with its impressive Great Hall (1906-9), now named after its architect. He also carried out work for the Imperial War Graves Commission, as well as designing war memorials like that outside the Royal Exchange in London.

Aston Webb designed churches as varied as St George's, Worcester, and the French Protestant Church in Soho Square, as well as the Methodist Central Hall in Westminster, and the reredos of St John's church, Notting Hill. He built schools and colleges, notably Christ's Hospital in Horsham, Sussex (1893-1902), the Imperial College of Science, South Kensington (1900-1906) of which only the tower now survives, King's College, Cambridge (1908), the Royal School of Mines, South Kensington (1909-1913), Worth School, West Sussex and Royal Russell School, Coombe, Croydon, Surrey. He also found time to accept commissions for other private houses besides "Brackenwood", such as a group of Arts & Crafts style cottages at Paddockhurst in Sussex, and Nos 2 (The Gables) and 4 (Windermere) Blackheath Park, in Blackheath, south-east London.

In 1890 he moved to No 1 Hanover Terrace (now No 1 Lansdowne Walk), which was to be his family's home for the rest of his life. The house was remodelled by him in 1900 in

Above:
Blackenwood

Left:
The former
Evans Medical
factory Wood St.,
Liverpool, designed
by Aston Webb

the Arts & Crafts style, and includes a plaster moulding of a spider's web, complete with spider and fly, a visual pun on his name.

Webb was knighted in 1904, received the Royal Gold Medal for Architecture in 1905 and was the first recipient of the American Institute of Architects Gold Medal in 1907. Towards the end of his career he was joined in his practice by his sons, Maurice and Philip. There are two portraits of him in the National Portrait Gallery, one by Sir William Rothenstein, the other by Solomon Joseph Solomon.

Webb died in1930 and is buried in Gunnersbury Cemetery, London. Like other presidents of the Royal Academy, he is remembered in St. Paul's Cathedral, with a wall tablet near the tomb of Sir Christopher Wren.

"Brackenwood" itself had a long carriage drive, its entrance guarded by a small gatekeeper's lodge, which still survives, on the corner of Bracken Lane and Brackenwood Road. The extensive gardens and grounds of the house stretched south along Mount Road towards Brimstage Road. The house occupied the crest of the sandstone ridge and from its lofty position commanded superb views towards Poulton Lancelyn and the hills of North Wales.

In 1920 the property was purchased by the then Bebington Urban Council, and it was used as council offices for many years. When Bebington Golf Club was closed in 1935, its members moved to Brackenwood Park, where a new nine-hole course had been laid out. The course was shared by the Bebington and Brackenwood Golf Clubs and the 'Oak Room' in Brackenwood House was used as a joint clubroom.

During the Second World War the fairways were ploughed up as part of the 'Dig for Victory' campaign, and used to grow vegetables. The course was not reinstated until 1946, by which time "Brackenwood" was suffering from the neglect of the war years. The Urban Council had many more urgent problems to address after the war, and the house fell into disrepair. In 1954, when it became unsafe to use the house, the golf clubhouse was relocated to part of the hayloft above the former stables behind "Brackenwood". The Council tried, unsuccessfully, to find other uses for the main house but, after a survey in 1958 had identified extensive dry rot, it was decided to demolish the house.

Although large Victorian and Edwardian houses were not greatly appreciated at that time, it is still astonishing that, apparently, nobody made the connection between this particular house and the architect of many major buildings, which have formed the backdrop to some of the most memorable occasions in the life of the nation. If more thought had been given to the significance of "Brackenwood", it might today have been one of the most distinguished buildings on Wirral. As it is, some of the small outbuildings remain, and the imposing raised terrace still overlooks a lawned area which was laid out as a putting green when John Evans and his family still occupied the house. All that remained of the house itself, at least until a few years ago, were some sections of window surrounds and other stones half buried and hidden in long grass close to Mount Road. Another survival is "Bracken Cottage" in Bracken Lane, which was built in 1904 for the Evans' coachman, and later renamed "Little House".

As a postscript; in the early 1970s Wirral Borough Council,

which had absorbed Bebington Urban Council, bought Needwood Farm, on the far side of the lower part of Brackenwood Road, from Lord Leverhulme and extended the golf course to 18 holes. The course was formally reopened in 1976. The golf club also negotiated a lease for the whole of the former stables and assumed responsibility for its maintenance. The old Needwood farmhouse, though not as imposing as "Brackenwood", was also demolished, although hedges still enclose its former site at the top of an unmade track off Brackenwood Road.

◆

Acknowledgments

I am happy to acknowledge a debt of gratitude to the following people and institutions. Researching such a wide range and diversity of subjects has involved locating many small snippets of information, the contribution of which to the wider picture should not be underestimated but, equally, may not be specifically mentioned, for which I can only apologise.

A Place for Everyone: The Scout Association of the United Kingdom; "A Topographical Dictionary of England, 7th Edition (1848); John Owen (http://vwlowen.co.uk/wirral); Wirral Metropolitan Borough Council, "The Wirral", Alan Brack. **Secrets of our Ancestors:** The Merseyside Archaeological Service, National Museums Liverpool; "Mesolithic Britain", C E Stone 2004 (www.portfolio.indy-net.co.uk/mesobrit). **A Tower More Elegant than Blackpool's:** Diane Stewart (http://easyweb.easynet.co.uk/~dstewart); National Museums Liverpool; New Brighton Community Partnership; Metropolitan Borough of Wirral. **The Forts of Liverpool Bay:** Bob Le-Roi; Frank Turner; Hywel Williams; "Lancashire Airfields in the Second World War", Aldon P. Ferguson; Martin Johns (www.whitstablescene.co.uk). **A Mariners' Floating Church:** "Ships of the Old Navy: A history of the sailing ships of the Royal Navy", Michael Phillips (www.cronab.demon.co.uk); Merseyside Maritime Museum; "Imperial Gazetteer of England & Wales" (1872), John Marius Wilson; "A History of the County of Lancaster", Volume 4, (1911); "The Art of W G Herdman", Kay Parrott, Bluecoat Press. **Pieces of History Sent Down the Slipway:** List of vessels constructed by Cammell Laird shipbuilders, Wirral Archives, Wirral MBC. **Wirral Fortifications:** "The Archaeology of World War II", Malcolm Atkin, Worcestershire Historic Environment and Archaeology Service; Pillbox Study Group, Graham G Matthews (www.pillbox-study-group.org.uk); "A Review of the Defence of Britain Project" (2002), British Council for Archaeology. **From Saxon Thanes to Vauxhall Motors:** Stuart Wilson, Mark Lewis, Matthew Roberts, Whitby High School, Ellesmere Port; Graham Michael Drake (www.drakesvision.com); PortCities Liverpool (www.mersey-gateway.org); "A Topographical Dictionary of England" (1848). **A Fighter in Miniature:** Aviation Metalcraft, Unit 28, Enterprise House, King Edward Street, Grimsby; Shuttleworth Collection, Old Warden Park, Bedfordshire; Hooton Park Trust, The Hangars, Hooton Park Airfield, Ellesmere Port; www.rochesterairport.

flyer.co.uk; Church of St Michael and All Angels, Inverness. **A Mediaeval Sailors' Hospital:** "A History of the County of Chester", Volume 3 (1980); Cheshire Archaeology News, Issue 6, Spring 1999; Burton Conservation Area Character Appraisal, Ellesmere Port & Neston Borough Council; "The Monastic and Religious Orders in the Hundred of Wirral from the Saxons to the Dissolution of the Monasteries - a study of the Monastic history and heritage of Wirral", Norman Blake; "Monastic and Collegiate Cheshire", R W Morant. **Hard Times and the Birth of a Legend:** "Wyrale", Greg Dawson (1996); "England's Mistress: the infamous life of Emma Hamilton", Kate Williams (2006); Evidence to EP&NBC Planning Committee, 14/02/06, The 1805 Club. **Straining Towards the Heavens:** "Heswall Friends", John Noble, Religious Society of Friends, Heswall Preparative Meeting (1988); "Buildings of Cheshire", Nikolaus Pevsner; Dewi Prys Thomas papers, National Library of Wales. **Flat Water, Strong Winds:** Hoylake/West Kirby Masterplan - 'The Sail', Wirral MBC (2004); History of West Kirby Sailing Club (http://www.wksc.net). **Waterways That Are and Aren't:** "Lost Canals & Waterways of Britain", Ronald Russell (1982); "The Complete Book of Canal and River Navigations", E Paget-Tomlinson (1984); "Navigable Waterways", L T C Rolt (1969); "Historical Account of the Navigable Rivers, Canals and Railways Throughout Great Britain", Joseph Priestley (1831); Mike Stevens (www.mike-stevens.co.uk). **Not Too Bad a Place To Be:** "A Short History of the Clatterbridge Hospitals", Central Wirral Hospital Management Committee (1966); Peter· Higginbotham (users.ox.ac.uk/~peter/workhouse/Wirral); Wirral Workhouse, 1881 Census. **A Lost Architectural Treasure:** Tina Bird (www.precision-guesswork.com); Newsletter, NW Branch Institute of Historic Building Conservation, June 2002; Celltech Group History (www.celltechgroup.com); History of Brackenwood Golf Club (http://brackenwoodgolfclub.co.uk). **General:** "The Search for Old Wirral", David Randall (1984); "The History of the County Palatine and City of Chester", G Ormerod (2nd Edition 1882); "The History of the Hundred of Wirral", W W Mortimer (1847).

Photographs

I am grateful to the following for their kind permission to make use of the following photographs:

Secrets of our Ancestors: Chert tool: City of Emeryville South Bayfront Project, California. **A Mediaeval Sailors' Hospital:** St Cross, Winchester: Allan Soedring; Norman sawtooth decoration: East Riding of Yorkshire Council. **Straining Towards the Heavens:** Telegraph Road c 1961: Heswall Preparative Meeting, Religious Society of Friends (Quakers). **A Lost Architectural Treasure:** Evans Medical factory, Wood Street, Liverpool: North West Branch, Institute of Historical Building Conservation.

I have been unable to trace the origins of the following photographs, all of which appear to be in the public domain:

A Place for Everyone: Baden-Powell. **Secrets of our Ancestors:** A Mesolithic hut. **A Tower More Elegant than Blackpool's:** New Brighton Tower from the sea. **The Forts of Liverpool Bay:** Mersey Fort; Towers under construction, Bromborough. **A Mariners' Floating Church:** George's Dock. **Pieces of History Sent Down the Slipway:** USS 'Kearsarge' and CSS 'Alabama'. **From Saxon Thanes to Vauxhall Motors:** Liverpool Mayor Margaret Beavan at Hooton; Hooton Hall. **A Fighter in Miniature:** Comper Swift advertisement; Charles Butler reaches Sydney, 1931. **Hard Times and the Birth of a Legend:** Last shift at Denhall Colliery. **Not Too Bad a Place To Be:** Workhouse stone yard. **A Lost Architectural Treasure:** Brackenwood House.

All other photographs are mine or come from the J J Hughes Archive which is in my possession.